Model Building

for

Decision Analysis

Model Building

for

Decision Analysis

PATRICK RIVETT

Professor of Operational Research, University of Sussex

JOHN WILEY & SONS
Chichester · New York · Brisbane · Toronto

British Library Cataloguing in Publication Data:

Rivett, Patrick
  Model building for decision analysis.
  1. Decision-making—Statistical models
  I. Title
  658.4'03   HD30.23   79-40739

  ISBN 0 471 27654 5

Phototypeset by Dobbie Typesetting Service, Plymouth, Devon, England
Printed by Page Bros (Norwich) Ltd., Mile Cross Lane, Norwich.

For

ANN, SHEILA, DAVID, ANDREW and CAROLINE

Preface

MODEL construction is an amalgam of theory and practice in which, unfortunately, either theory or practice appears from time to time as the dominant constituent. When theory is dominant, elegance of mathematical exposition may lead to consequences which are incapable of implementation. On the other hand hurried problem solving which conceals within it a technical ineptitude may mean that insight into the structure is lost. Between these two extremes there lies a depopulated no man's land. A false distinction and a sham battle between the 'pure' and the 'applied' has meant that the pure have produced their theories and the applied their practice, in two different incommunicating languages.

This book seeks to explore this middle ground. I assume that the reader has an understanding of basic statistics and of the usual mathematical techniques of Operational Research. It is, of course, inevitable that those who use this book will find that the boundary of technical knowledge which I have assumed, does not match their own, but I have tried to take as starting conditions the basic knowledge which most operational research and management scientists possess. In the book I seek to explore the stages by which decision models may be constructed and subject the techniques to what I hope is a constructive criticism. I hope my readers will not think the criticism is too destructive but it is in some cases necessary to offer some antidote to the great enthusiasm with which some technique approaches have been evangelized.

This book is a development of an earlier book published in 1972 entitled *Principles of Model Building*. In 1965, when I was at the University of Lancaster, we tried the then daring experiment of trying to teach model building to our M.Sc. students or, as we put it, what goes on in an analyst's head when he is taken round a soap factory? At that time all of three lectures were devoted to this.

As time went on the material expanded like the brooms in the Sorcerer's Apprentice. When I came to Sussex in 1967 the material was covered in ten lectures, and at this time (1979) we are reorganising our masters course to incorporate approximately 40 hours on model building and even this may not be enough.

This development has not been (solely) due to the author's increasing garrulity with the onset of age but rather to the interaction of successive years of lively, articulate and interesting students and of the natural stretching process that occurs when one is put on the rack by one's colleagues and friends. (These are not mutually exclusive categories!) I owe a debt to all of these, both students and academic colleagues. My own research has led to the enlargement of the sections on multiple criteria decision making, while the research of my colleagues has led to other enlargements. I am particularly grateful to Dr. Peter Bennett of Sussex University for the section on hyper game analysis.

No one indeed writes a book alone in a cell. I also owe a debt to many friends, particularly Professors Russ Ackoff, Stafford Beer, West Churchman, David Hertz and Keith Tocher. The chapters on competition and accounting were worked through respectively by Professor Alan Mercer and Jeremy Roberts.

Thanks are due to the Editor of the *Proceedings of the Royal Society* of London for permission to reproduce the diagram on page 153 and to the Editor of *Omega* for permission to reproduce material from a paper of mine in the chapter on Forecasting.

Finally, I would like to thank my secretary, Mrs. Diane Austin, who has typed successive versions of this book so often that she can recite most of it by heart.

PATRICK RIVETT

University of Sussex,.
Brighton, 1979

Contents

1 The Model in Science

'In simplicity we had our conversation'

St. Paul

The model in history

All scientists are aware that the central act of the scientific method is the creation of a model. The concept of model building has, particularly in recent years, become clothed in some form of mystique and yet the whole history of man, even in his most non-scientific activities, shows that he is essentially a model-building animal. A model is first of all a convenient way of representing the total experience which we possess, of then deducing from that experience whether we are in the presence of pattern and law and, if so, of showing how such patterns and laws can be used to predict the future. It might even be said that the proverb 'red sky at night, shepherds' delight; red sky in the morning, shepherds' warning' is a form of model in which the objective is implicitly stated.

It is natural that operational research scientists, and others who are concerned with creating understanding of the decision-making process, should seek to do so by means of model building. The concept of modelling sets off these quantitative structured sciences from other forms of approach to management decision-making. Unfortunately some more enthusiastic model builders have hailed the concept of the model as a unique contribution that operational research has made to the mainstream of the scientific method. This is nonsense.

It is of interest to see how man's concept of modelling has developed over the centuries, with particular reference to a field which has interested him from his earliest days on earth—namely, that of studying and forecasting the movement of stars and planets. The discovery of the archives of the great cities of Mesopotamia revealed that from its earliest days the Babylonian civilization had preserved legibly a mass of records in cuneiform script, that is wedge-shaped impressions made by a stick in a soft clay which was subsequently baked in order to preserve the indentations.[1]

The earliest tablets cover matters of law and ritual and give inventories of cattle, slaves and crops. They also incorporate the names of their gods, which were also the names of the heavenly bodies. These comprised, and developed into, a series of planetary observations (that is, tables which were used to predict the motions and eclipses of the moon) and arithmetical texts on how to calculate the daily positions of the planets, times and dates of earthquakes, plagues of locusts and other natural disasters. In all this man's search for recurrent cycle and pattern was evident. We all have questions about the nature of the universe in which we live and one form of question is to ask whether we are subject to pattern or in the grip of blind chaos. At the end of *Tess of the D'Urbervilles*, Hardy sums up this desperate feeling of being in the grip of chaos in the sentence 'the President of the Immortals . . . had ended his sport with Tess'. The model builder looks for something beyond blind sport.

The history of man, then, is a history of model building. It is a history of a constant search for pattern and for generalization. The Babylonians kept continuous dated records of a whole series of celestial events for a period of over 600 years, starting from about 750 BC. At the beginning, measurement was of necessity rough and approximate: something of the order of 'three finger breadths to the left of the great planet' was sufficient an indication. However, midway through this period there was the development of degrees. The sky was divided into the signs of the zodiac with twelve zones, each of thirty degrees. The Babylonian number system was on a base of sixty. This is the reason why even today we have minutes and seconds on a base of 60 used in degree measure.

The methods employed by the Babylonians for analysing cycle and trend were the elementary methods of statistical analysis. The basic concept was that of a long term trend on which was superimposed a cyclic event. These methods could forecast celestial movements with great precision. Even without the use of telescopes and accurate measuring instruments they were able to predict accurately and the late Babylonian astronomer, Kidinmu, in about 300 BC estimated the value for the motion of the sun from the node with an error of only five seconds. In the nineteenth century the astronomer Hansen only managed to do this with an error of seven seconds. The reason was that the Babylonians had 600 years of data, which was vastly more than Hansen possessed, and it illustrates the well-known statistical point that accuracy of data is not necessarily more important than extent of data. Hence the precision of the estimate we develop is not solely related to the precision with which the observations are carried out.

On looking back at this history of Babylonian record-keeping we can see a number of interesting features which underpin so much of management control data today. Extreme care was taken in record-keeping, rather akin to the careful and detailed records that accountants will provide. There was mathematical brilliance of prediction, much akin in its depth and penetration to modern statistical methods. However, there was no explanation of why things occurred and nothing was more intelligible after the data and predictions were provided than it was before. Again, much modern management control data suffers from this defect. It is intriguing to ask the question, why the Babylonians did not theorize, why they did not build up models which were explanatory in nature rather than merely predictive? Perhaps the reason was that the stars which they were studying were gods; to them it was enough and sufficient to predict the behaviour of the gods. It would have been impertinent to try and explain the behaviour of gods. Until the advent of behavioural sciences it is perhaps true to say that much of management research has had the same view of our present gods of management, namely that it is enough to be able to predict what the boards of companies would want, and even what the shareholders might want, but that it would be impertinent to seek to explain why they should want it.

The beginnings of the Greek interest in astronomy overlapped the end of the Babylonian era but they did not possess the Babylonian data. Aristotle had, previous to the conquest of Babylon, proposed a mechanical procedure for planetary motion in which the planets were envisaged as being on the circumference of 27 spheres, consisting of three concentric spheres and the remainder of 24 in the interstices. It is interesting to note that from the beginning the approach of the Greeks was to seek to explain by means of some form of mechanical analogy rather than solely to predict. The Babylonian data, when it was discovered, showed that such a mechanical analogy was unusable. Ptolemy had used geometrical approaches to replace the arithmetic of the Babylonians, to show that by three devices, the epicycle, the eccentric and the equant, the path of the sun, moon and five other planets could be forecast accurately. However, he built a separate construction of circles for each planet and he produced separate constructions to deal with different aspects of the same planet. For example the moon's speed and its changes of diameter were forecast and estimated by quite separate constructions. Nowhere did Ptolemy succeed in unifying, and whenever two constructions yielded the same mathematical result he assumed there was no astronomical difference between them. It is perhaps a sad commentary on some contemporary model building for decision-making that we make the same assumption; that if two mathematical constructions yield the same result we assume that there is no philosophical or managerial difference between the two constructions.

Any attempt to devise a gravitational law, as was proposed by Newton, would have been impossible to deal with, even with today's largest computers, without Newton's simplifying law that the gravitational attraction of the body can be regarded as located as its centre of gravity. The inverse square law of attraction can be regarded as an explanatory statement, *prima facie*, and yet, why a square law and not a cube law? It is interesting in passing to reflect on the minimum number of constants which need to exist in the world. Given our present knowledge of the physical world the speed of sound at sea level is, for example, a fixed quantity. The experiments which were devoted to estimating the speed of sound were quite redundant, given our present day knowledge of the total mechanism. Explanatory laws are often therefore merely descriptive laws which have been taken to a higher level. What Newton's law achieved was what we seek from all model-building laws. They unify. By means of a many-one transformation they simplified. They could be used for prediction and subjected to continuous check. Indeed, as can be seen from the Babylonian and Greek approaches, a model can be predictive without being explanatory (the Babylonian) but an explanatory model must be predictive (e.g. the Greek). A model which is merely predictive works within narrow confines, yields no understanding, neither does it provide of itself any means of checking when the underlying logic has changed significantly. In addition, the distinction which Ackoff makes[2] between the three *forms* of model (iconic, analogic and analytic) should be noted. In later chapters we use an explicitly mathematical relation as a shorthand for a model. However, it should be observed that the mathematical relationship is using mathematics as a language to describe functional relationship which may be iconic or analogic rather than necessarily analytic.

Of course, to talk of a scientific law is rather dangerous. A scientific 'law' is merely a scientific hypothesis which has not yet been disproved. Newton's laws are an example both of this and of the great power of prediction which stems from a law. For example, in the 1840s, perturbations had been noted in the orbit of the planet Uranus. An explanation which could fit these observations was that there was another unknown planet, called Neptune. On a given day, the telescope in Berlin was aligned in the correct direction at the correct time, and there indeed was the new and previously unobserved planet, Neptune. (This is a powerful example of the way in which a scientific law, when proposed, can be used to show reasons for an apparent breakdown in the law. Indeed when fresh facts fail to fit a hypothesis, we always have to ask three questions: is the hypothesis now disproved; are there certain things which we have neglected to take account of; are the facts themselves correct?) Later, Mercury showed irregularity in its axis of orbit and a similar explanation of a new planet, called Vulcan, was proposed. Vulcan has never yet been proved to exist and these irregularities in Mercury led to the proposal by Einstein of the general theory of relativity which involves slight changes in the Newtonian law, but whether the general theory explains the deviations in Mercury is still open to question.

The scientific method

It is commonplace to aver that the scientific method consists of a number of stages. The basic stages are four: observation, generalization, experimentation and validation. This often extended and formalized to fit the processes of operational research:

> formulation of the problem;
> constsructing a model;
> deriving a solution;
> testing and controlling the solution;
> implementing the solution.

Clearly, this process is cyclic and the series of steps overlap with each other. However, it must be made clear that in this formulation of the method there must be a statement of the objectives involved, since formulating the problem without formulating the objectives may mean we solve for symptoms only.

It will be the thesis of a later chapter that objectives cannot be treated separately from the model formulation. In some cases, moreover, the idea of a model and the idea of an objective function are completely confounded and the form by which the model is stated is in fact that of an objective function. The inter-relationship of the objective function and of the model is subtle and intricate but one has to be quite clear about the way in which they differ. It will be part of the purpose of this book to seek to make clear this distinction and also to show the way in which they interact on each other.

What is it that goes on in the mind of the operational research scientist when he first comes to a new problem? What goes on in his mind when for the first time he walks around the soap factory at Leeds? Is he seeking for some 'best' model?

Clearly, one observes that there is no such thing as a unique 'best' model for any management situation. There are some operational research groups which concentrate on building models which are solely of a linear programming type. There are others which build models solely of a simulation nature. Now, either these groups are being faced with a very peculiar subset of problems which have this continuity of technique associated with them, or there will be a variety of model-building approaches which can be used and such groups will use models which from their experience they are most likely to be able to solve.

There is indeed a very interesting problem to be faced here. Most operational research scientists maintain, with reason, that the formulation and solution of the problem must dominate the selection of any particular set of techniques which are used. This is certainly the case but, as Medawar has pointed out elsewhere,[3] there is no credit to be gained in scientific research from failing to solve a problem. Scientists have always selected, and will continue to select, problems which they feel capable of solving. Hence, in the first stages of an operational research study the research scientist has a knowledge of those approaches with which he feels most competent to deal, and there will be a temptation for him to formulate the problem in the image of these approaches (as will be seen in a later chapter). This introduces the idea and the problem of objective constrained and objective free modelling, which is not often under-stood as an important point in the model-building process.

However, even before the stage at which the research scientist is formulating in his mind particular thoughts of the type of model he might use, there is yet another cause of variablity in approach. This is that when two research scientists walk at the same time around the soap factory at Leeds we have no means at all of understanding what the common elements are in what they see or what the relative importances are to each of them personally of the things they see. Consequently, at its very first point operational research is a subjective personal science. From this first subjective personal approach we are each of us influenced by forms of modelling which are attractive to us and hence there is no reason to be surprised at the variety of approaches which can be taken, and are taken, to similar problems. Unfortunately the situation in which the research scientist finds himself means that it is impossible to carry out any comparative operational research. By this we mean that if one research team studies a problem and proposes a particular form of model for it, there is no possibility of another team then taking the same problem in the same organization and building a second model, and for the two to be compared in effectiveness. The Heisenberg effect dominates the situation and comparative operational research of this nature is quite impossible.

Model building

So far we have discussed the background of the scientific method which the scientist will carry into every decision-making situation, together with some of the difficulties involved in formulating comparative approaches. However, it can be stated that there is a view of the whole process of modelling which should inform all approaches and one such view is proposed in Figure 1.

Some of the points which stem from the study of Figure 1 might be of interest because they affect some of the basic beliefs which are held by the research scientist.

A. We are concerned, in model building, with some understanding and concept of what we like to call 'reality'. To discuss aspects of reality is to admit important and deep philosophical problems which lie beyond the scope of this book. However, we can say three things about this reality with which we are concerned. They are that it is observable, measurable and systemic.

By observable we mean that it is possible for the research scientist to see some aspects of what is going on, for him to try and understand the characteristics of these aspects and to be able to build some form of predictor not only of behaviour but also, as can be seen at a later stage, to compare the results of this hypothesis with this reality by making further observations. These observations may sometimes be in the form of specific scientific or statistically controlled experiments. In operational research we are concerned not so much with trial and error as with trial and catastrophe, as the consequences of experimenting with a system may well be punitive. Consequently in most cases we are observing at arm's length and not interfering with the system. This is one reason why operational research never has been and probably never will be a field of endeavour for the classical statistician, using only classical statistical methods of experimental design.

As has been implied in the above, another criterion of the reality which we observe is that certain aspects of it should be measurable. Some contemporary operational research is being carried out in fields where measurement is not possible. These include problems to which we shall return in Chapters 6 and 7 where we are estimating the probabilities of events which have never yet had a chance to occur. Apart, however, from these situations which are subject to some question and criticism in any event, we depend on measurement. The one thing which a research scientist in general will not bring to

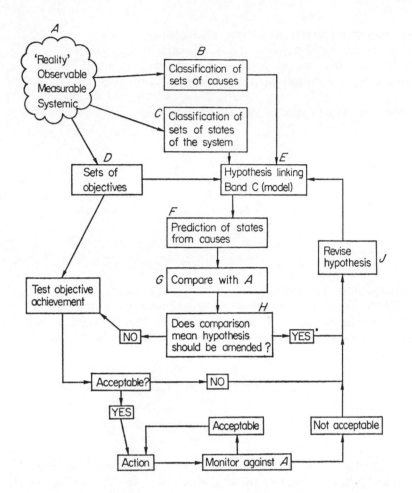

Figure 1. The model-building process

any management situation which he is studying is any form of experience of handling that system.

The third characteristic of this reality is that it is, to use Beer's phrase, systemic. By this we mean that there is a set of causes and set of effects interacting in a complex manner, simultaneously. This is another reason why routine statistical methods of application are difficult within the field of operational research. The idea of the systemic nature of the reality to which we refer is fully explored by Beer in his paper[4] and also in *Decision and Control*.[5]

However, an outline of the concept is essential for the development of the argument of this section. A system consists of a set of entities with three properties:

(a) Every entity affects at least one other entity in the set.
(b) Every entity is affected by at least one other entity in the set.
(c) The set cannot be split into two sub-sets, with no member of one set not affected by or not affecting at least one member of the other.

Hence a simple system of two entities might be:

This is the only possible system of two entities and corresponds to an elementary feedback loop. In particular one is well aware of:

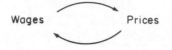

An example of a three-part system is that of a shepherd, a dog and a flock of sheep. We can take a many-one transformation and replace the flock of sheep by one sheep. From the view point of the shepherd, as master, if '————' represents information (which carries within it an effect on the receiver)

From the view point of the dog, as master, he can act so as to make the shepherd whistle whenever the dog wants him to, by moving the sheep.

Finally the sheep can regard themselves as the complete master by causing the shepherd to whistle and the dog to respond.

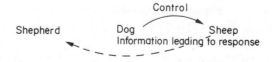

The point is that on evidence of observations of the Shepherd-Dog-Sheep trinity it is impossible to know who is the boss. To do this one would have to be able to carry out controlled experiments. This is true of all systems and has the important consequence that formal optimisation procedures are unlikely to 'solve' a systemic problem unless we can understand the internal processes of the nature of cause-effect within the system.

A fairly common industrial example of a system has as its archetype the lorry convoy problem. A chain of lorries is driving along a straight road, each driver attempting to keep a constant distance from the vehicle in front. Small perturbations in the speed of the leading vehicle are transformed down through the convoy into larger and larger perturbations; anyone who has observed a long procession like the Lord Mayor's show, will be familiar with this. The man on the white horse at the front travels at (approximately) constant speed; the troops at the rear spend time standing easy or moving at the double. The industrial parallel is the ordering of inventories. Small changes in the rate of demand for a finished product, when translated into successive larger orders for components back through the system, gives a feast-famine situation at the basic raw material supplier. In parallel with this is the increasing fluctuation of costs as one moves back from the ultimate consumer to the prime supplier, it being difficult in some cases to know whether these two phenomena are related or independent.

Finally, when contemplating a system, it is difficult to know where the boundary should be set. It seemed clear for the Shepherd-Dog-Sheep example; it is not so clear with the chain of lorries. For most real-life problems, the creation of the boundary is an essential determinant of the form of solution which will be obtained.

B. Depending on where the boundary is drawn and on the objectives of the study, we can formulate a set of causes. Many of these may have to be grouped together if we are to be able to cope with the analytical problems. For example, in share price problems we might use an average price for all electrical manufacturing shares, rather than separate prices for each share. Even a more coarse grouping might be necessary in some cases, where the *Financial Times* index might represent the whole market. The critical feature is the objective of the research. For example, if the study relates to a production shop, then the ages and domestic circumstances of the work force would be a causal variable if the objective was labour wastage from the shop, but would be omitted altogether in a conventional linear programme aimed at allocating orders to machines to maximise contribution to profit.

C. The system we are observing will, in general, be continuous in nature but in some cases it may change through step-function jumps. In either case we have to be able to describe the present state of the system at any time. Again, the richness involved is such that we cannot hope to consider and tabulate every bit of information and hence the system may be classified rather than described.

In addition, the description of the system is affected by, and itself affects, the methods or techniques of the investigation. For example, if in a queueing problem it is found that the interval between arrivals has a negative exponential distribution, then we know that the probability distribution of the time to the next arrival is independent of the time since the last arrival. In addition, if the service time has the same form of distribution, then the probability distribution of the time elapsing until the occupant of the service point is ejected is independent of the time it has already been in service. Consequently the description of the system at any time will, for the single queue without priority—single service point, exclude any use of the time since last arrival in the queue and last entry to service and consist solely of one number—the number of items in the system.

D. At the very centre of the diagram is the problem of the sets of objectives. As has been mentioned previously, we often neglect to consider what the objectives are in these early stages of model building. Frequently objectives are not realized until the end of the process of model building. If this is the case, then the looping back which is shown in Figure 1 has to take place so that objectives can be reformulated. The study of objectives is, curiously enough, one which has only recently come to the fore in operational research. We have in general been happy to receive objectives as being given to us by executives and managers and there has, as will be shown later, been little work in developing a formal calculus for dealing with sets of objectives.

The methods fall historically into three different categories, each making axiomatic demands of varying strength, namely cost-benefit analysis, linear programming and utility theory. As will be seen, however, in Chapter 12 there is the possibility of an approach with very weak axiomatic requirements using multi-dimension scaling techniques.

E. The three inputs of sets of causes, sets of states, sets of objectives are linked together by means of a basic hypothesis. This hypothesis will often be formulated as a logical qualitative statement and will be separate from quantitative data analysis. Sometimes, as will be seen, hypotheses are devised as a result of massive data analysis. In these cases we have to be careful before assigning credibility to a hypothesis devised in an unthinking way. This hypothesis as at E is what is termed the model.

The construction of a model is a matter of art, as much as science, that is to say it is something to be learnt from experience as much as by following a formal process. Since our view of the world is subjective, since also there is, *a priori*, no reason why one set of causes and effects should be of more merit than any other, then the model when it is formulated for the first time is both subjective and tentative. It is for this first model to survive intact the process of validation. It is, of course, common practice for the first model to be similar to other models and hence they tend to fall into classes, as suggested in Chapter 4.

F. Models are not derived solely so that some aspect of affairs might be better described. They are derived so that some complex situation might be subject to prediction and control, that is, the model must first of all be useful. This means that the first stage must be to satisfy ourselves of the potential usefulness of the model first of all by examining how well it predicts, that is how accurately does it tell us what states of the system (*C*) should result from different sets of causes (*B*). It will not be until the third stage that we examine the usefulness of the model in terms of objective achievement.

G. In between these first and third stages is this second stage which links the prediction of system states (*C*) with the 'reality' at (*A*). This is in itself a check on the validity of the classification used in (*B*) and (*C*) and is obviously dependent on statistical methods of hypothesis testing.

H. If these differences are not strong enough for the hypothesis to be rejected then we must test them against the set of objectives *D* to see whether the course of action is going to affect and improve the degree of attainment of the objective. If it is not, then we have to loop back into *J* in the same way that we shall have to loop back if, at *G* and *H*, the differences between prediction and reality are too great to be explained by chance causes.

The other alternative at the stage *H* will stem from the situation when the course of action is going to affect the objective attainment in a significant manner and then this course of action can be followed but with continuing checking, feeding in again at *F*.

The model and the objective function

The major part of the remainder of this book will be devoted to an attempt to show the way in which various parts of the above routine which should be followed, will be achieved by means of different standard approaches. We shall subject these approaches to some criticism but hope that such criticism will be in a positive and helpful manner.

As can be seen therefore, the model or hypothesis is a set of logical relationships, either qualitative or quantitative, which will link together the relevant features of the reality with which we are concerned. Such a logical statement can be expressed in the symbolic form

$$f(x_1, x_2 \ldots x_m; y_1, y_2 \ldots y_n).$$

It should be carefully noted that although such a statement implies, or even explicitly states, a mathematical formula, this is not necessarily the case. Neither is it the case that there will be only one such logical statement.

In this statement we assume that the *x*'s are controllable factors while the *y*'s are uncontrollable. Of course, once one states 'controllable', one has to ask by whom? It is not the case that at every level of an organization there is a progression of controllable factors as one moves from the base towards the apex. At any level of management those in office at that level will retain to themselves that set of decision which, out of all those they are allowed, is the most sensitive in their opinion, while delegating to those below them the less sensitive parts of their job. This delegation implies a rapid degradation of control as one moves down the organization from the original delegator. Hence one can think in terms of a man on a particular level being able to control what goes on at perhaps two levels below him and being able to influence what goes on at up to two levels above him. This, of course, is not an explicit law of organizations, but it is one in which there is some justification.

The factors grouped together under the heading y are those which are uncontrollable. They are of two kinds. There are those factors which are naturally uncontrollable in the sense that they belong essentially to nature. These will be the general state of the economy, raw material prices, laws, social ethos, and so on. The other factors in this set are those which are controllable by an opponent who is not devoted to one's own well-being. As will be seen in the section on the competitive models, when the response of an opponent to one's own controllable variables is sluggish, then this set of variables which are controllable by the opponent can be subsumed with nature, without affecting the model-making procedure.

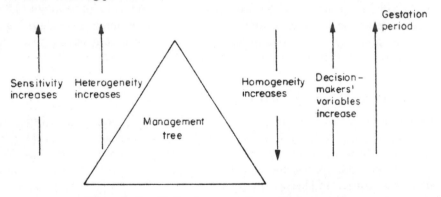

Figure 2. Sensitivity, homogeneity and heterogeneity

As one proceeds down the management tree, it can also be seen that the variables with which the decision-makers could be concerned become more homogeneous in nature and fewer in number. Hence, at the junior levels in an organization the controllable variables are relatively few, the variables concerned in the model are homogeneous and can be measured in terms of the same unit. As one proceeds up the organization towards the top, the number of variables which the decision-maker can affect are greater; there is even perhaps the possibility of doing something about controlling nature itself and in addition the variables become far more heterogeneous in nature and the homogeneity which makes decision-making at the lower levels of organizations so attractive, begins to disappear. We note however the 'could be' above. In practical management terms those at the top may select only a few variables with which to be concerned. This is their choice, however, and they may if they wish be concerned with everything.

The objectives of the organization and the degree to which they are obtained can be expressed in a similar fashion to the model statement above. Hence we will have for an organization at least one, and possibly many, functions of the form

$$P = F(x_1, x_2, \ldots, x_p; y_1, y_2, \ldots, y_q)$$

where P is some measure of performance. Such a relation is called an objective function. Again in these functions the x's are controllable variables and the y's are the uncontrollables. The task of the decision-maker is to forecast the y's and then to select the x's in such a way that the objective function is maximised or minimized (as in the case of optimization) or made acceptable (as in the case of the satisfycing approach).

It is in the introduction of the objective function that the distinction is made between operational research models and those of the mainstream of science. Scientific models are always for prediction and understanding. The introduction of control as a reason for an operational research model immediately leads to the question of 'control for what?' The 'what' is given by the set of objective functions. Hence an understanding of objectives is a necessary condition for model construction in operational research.

The model, as built, will stem from the operational researcher's analysis of the experience of those with whom he is dealing within the organization and also from his own understanding of the general problem area, which he may have gained elsewhere. In general the first statement of the model will be in a qualitative logical fashion, in the form of a flow chart. The quantification which is implicit in the model is better done at a second stage. This is obtained by data trapping and collection and by testing the relevance and significance of the hypotheses which have been adduced in the model. This means that it is first necessary to understand what we might, in broad terms, call the technology of the management situation. This will certainly include the basic engineering and production technology if this is appropriate. It will also involve an understanding of the total situation of the organization, financial, marketing, production and purchasing, as well as an understanding of the total situation in terms of the motivations of those who are seeking to control it. This is why at the beginning of an operational research study, sometimes apparently nothing happens, because the team is engaged in a process of understanding which, of its nature, cannot be hurried. One sometimes has the impression that some operational research scientists can walk round the soap factory at Leeds and immediately decide that they are faced with a typical linear programming problem. Again one must emphasize that this first process of understanding is absolutely necessary for operational research, as in general the faster he tries to obtain an off-the-cuff understanding and answer, the more the operational research scientist is trying to work like a manager and he, the scientist, has not the skill, experience and intuition which the manager has gained in these situations.

Inductive and deductive models

Any model which is formed solely as the result of statistical or mathematical analysis, without any *a priori* consideration of what 'ought' to be happening is, as has been stated earlier, of the descriptive type. Also, because we start with evidence and form conclusions based on that evidence, it is deductive. The other form, the explanatory model, reverses the logical process and is inductive in form. In general, the amount of analysis necessary to confirm an explanatory or inductive model is less than for the other type, since this model draws for its credibility on evidence and experience already accumulated at other times or in other places. Hence in general they are more efficient.

Sometimes it is not possible to devise a basic logical model in a qualitative form before clothing it with number. It may be necessary to derive a structure from a statistical analysis. In these cases care and caution must be exercised. No operational research scientist needs reminding of nonsense correlations and their perils. Sometimes statistically derived models when devised will accord with common sense. In general one should be much happier about accepting models which accord with common sense, but it must be remembered that where one makes an error by accepting common sense which in fact is wrong, then the degree of loss to the organization is very great. By this we mean that when one can show that common sense has been a bad master there is a significant step-function-type gain to be obtained by the organization. Again we must be careful, because the operational research scientist, like all scientists, has a natural tendency to look for pattern and consistency and to assume that when he has got pattern or consistency then he has a grasp of the truth. Hence there is a danger that we may induce pattern where it does not exist.

Pattern recognition

Bavelas of Stanford University carried out a series of interesting experiments which show the danger of pattern induction. He presented individual graduate students each with a series of pictures which had a purely random pattern on them (the random pattern was obtained by random movement of a light source exposed on a photographic plate). He presented each one of these students with the random pictures one at a time and invited them to press one of two buttons. The task of the student was to deduce which was the correct button to press for each pattern. On the pressing of a button the student was told whether he was correct or in error, and whether he was told correct or in error was given by reference to a table of random numbers. In the presence of this complete random noise situation each student deduced eventually that he could determine when he should press the one button or when he should press the other. He was then asked to teach his method to other groups of students. Eventually when the students were told that the whole thing was a hoax, their response to the experiment was often 'you may think that these patterns were random, but we having observed them, know better'.

There is, therefore, constantly the danger that we may induce pattern because we feel that pattern is the natural state which must always be present. It may then be that when we observe a pattern within the data, our standards of judgement may be reduced because this is what we expect to find. There are other cases in which the model will run counter to common sense but then we should insist on a higher level of statistical conviction and proof than in those cases where the model accords with common sense. For example, if with the following series,

$$1860, 1880, 1900, 1920, 1940, 1960,$$

one was asked to predict the next number in the series, it would not be unreasonable to suggest that it might well be 1980. Indeed in the absence of any other information it is difficult to think of another prediction.

Now however, here is an additional piece of information. In the years listed above, the United States Presidential election was won respectively by Lincoln, Garfield, McKinley, Harding, Roosevelt and Kennedy. We observe that each one of these presidents died in office, and no president has died in office in the last century who did not win the election in one of those years. It is not necessarily now the case that we would predict that the next president to die in office would be the man who wins in 1980. On the other hand, if America were old enough for such a series to have been in existence for, say, 300 years one might very well reflect that although one could not explain the mechanism behind the series the statistical conviction of the data was now sufficient for us to accept a hypothesis which we could not explain, and for any one of us to decline the nomination in 1980.

As can be seen in the above example we have gone through the cycle of acceptance, rejection and acceptance of a hypothesis. Without the names of the Presidents 1980 was a fair prediction. The names of only six Presidents who died in office lead us to reject the hypothesis that 1980 will be the next number in the series. But there could be a level at which we cannot explain the casual connexion but are forced to accept it because of the overwhelming nature of the statistical data. The same argument has been followed in research into a causal relation between cigarette smoking and lung cancer where, at present, the physiological explanation is still lacking. This is a good example of another way in which we may be led to adopt a cause-effect relationship. To some it may appear that smoking cigarettes is a confession of weakness of character and it is only 'natural' that something so pleasant should carry a penalty. If cigarette smoking is shown statistically to increase energy and prolong active life, we may then require (from personal moral grounds) a higher level of statistical conviction than is at present accepted. (The author is not making any judgement on the statistical evidence for lung cancer but merely suggesting that acceptance of a hypothesis may depend on its palatability).

There is indeed a practical example of this danger of observing what is not present for which, unfortunately, the author was responsible. A company marketing a product not only had a salesforce responsible for selling the product to wholesalers but also had a group of sales servicemen whose responsibility was to visit retail outlets to ensure that the product was displayed effectively on the shelves of the retailer. The question was what was achieved by the sales servicemen?

It was possible to derive for each sales area (corresponding to the I.T.V. areas) an estimate of the number of retail outlets stocking the product, the number of these outlets called on by the sales servicemen and the share of market enjoyed by the product. This last was obtained by retail audits in a sample of stores in each area.

The data showed a pleasing relationship:

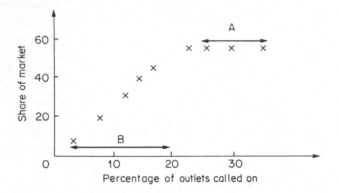

It seemed clear that there was an increasing relationship, moving to an asymptote at about 60%. It also seemed clear that a shift of servicemen from some of the areas A to the areas B would gain more sales in B than they would lose in A. Accordingly, the servicemen were moved from one area to another.

As the last of these domestic moves was completed the market research group of the company in question announced that they now had a new, and more accurate, method of estimating share of market based on a different sample of stores. Alas, on the basis of these new data we now had the relationship:

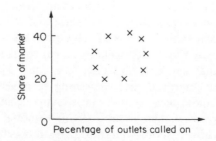

The moral of the story is that had the analysis yielded the second relationship one would have asked why? And the answer would have produced the information that market research were formulating a different method of estimating the parameters involved. But because a 'sensible' relationship emerged from the first analysis, no question was asked about the validity of the data.

The same parallel must apply in every situation where we are testing a hypothesis in model building. In general these hypotheses will be based on 'common sense'. The real breakthroughs are to be obtained when we can show common sense to be wrong, but in these situations we must demand, as an insurance against accepting something which is foolish, that the level of statistical evidence should be greater than in those situations where we observe what we expect to observe, namely something which corresponds to common sense.

2 Influences on the Decision-Taker

'Delilah pressed him daily with her words'
Book of Judges

Pressures on the system

Emphasis has already been placed on the need to understand the pressures which act on the organization as a whole, and also on the particular administrators within it whom the scientist is serving. Let us be quite clear at this stage of a point to which we shall return in a later chapter, namely that we have to move away from the simplistic view of an organization as being, if it is in any way commercially oriented, devoted solely to maximizing its profits or its profitability. In dealing with organizations, whether industrial, commercial, social or governmental, we are dealing with complex systems operating under a complex set of pressures in order to achieve ends and objectives which are ill-defined, ill-structured and possibly mutually conflicting. The task of management is difficult and not to be approached lightly. It is now useful to observe the pressures acting on a typical commercially oriented organization. Whatever the type of organization which is under study, the operational research scientist should at an early stage try to build up a similar statement which will show the environment within which the organization operates, for it is only through understanding the pressures acting on the organization and its individual decision-makers that we can understand the sets of objectives and goals and criteria which are involved. For each of these pressures there may well be a related measure of performance and hence a related objective function. In addition these pressures may act as constraints on the performance of the system and are reflected in constraints in the model.

The industrial company will act within a complex situation. It is placed, first of all, within a local community or a series of local communities, and its decision-making will be influenced by the need to act as a good neighbour within these communities. Not only is there a contemporary or future need for such good neighbour conduct, but past history will play a part in determining company policy. For example, there are some mines operated by the National Coal Board in Scotland and in South Wales which are always difficult to operate and have continual labour problems, not because of any action of the present management, but because of actions taken by private colliery companies as long as fifty years ago. The local community within which the company plays a part, and within which most of its employees will live and pay their rates and taxes, is a powerful conditioning factor in its operation.

Larger than the local community is the nation and its needs. Most companies are concerned with national well-being as well as their own organizational well-being. Most companies will try to respond to pleas from successive governments to export more, even though exporting as such may not be as profitable as selling within this country, but how far should a company sacrifice itself and its prospects to meet national needs which may sometimes be political rather than economic? How can national needs be understood in the absence of any explicit national consensus? This interaction between company and nation is delicate and intricate.

Nominally the organization is responsible to its owners in the form of its shareholders. Indeed some writers express a moral imperative to do nothing except to serve the interest of the owners. But only about twenty per cent of the capital of companies is supplied from equity shareholding, the remainder coming from large institutions or being ploughed back from profits, and hence the claim of the owners to exercise control over the company is somewhat tenuous. In my own experience of many years of working in many companies, I have never heard the shareholders mentioned as being a contributory factor to be taken into account in decision-making. There will obviously be pressures to keep up the price of the shares by high dividends, but this generally is not because of any feeling that the shareholders as such have rights to such dividends, but rather because one wants to retain a high enough price on the shares to deter would-be take-overs and also because one wants to preserve the possibility of raising more capital in the market on the basis of past company performance.

The financial analysts are becoming more important because of this need for the company shares to obtain proper standing in the market. In America a great deal of trouble is taken by companies to preserve their relations with financial analysts so that they are fully aware of any valid reasons for an apparent decline in a company performance in any one year. One can reflect in passing that, within the total context of a company, one year is a fleeting moment of time, decisions taken in the company will generally have impact over many years to come and the annual accounting in these terms is fairly irrelevant. Unfortunately the market does not recognise this and hence the need to preserve and create understanding from the analysts.

There are two homogeneous groups of people with whom the organization will have to deal. There will firstly be the non-professional labour. It is difficult to establish a firm boundary between professional and non-professional labour, but in general the non-professional will rely on some form of union backing in order to secure his conditions of service and pay, where the professional tends to work individually with the company in this respect. The impact of trade unions on decision-making in companies is profound, more usually of course at the micro level. This is a pity because the most sensitive feature in determining micro decisions are the macro decisions, which so often are ignored by unions as being outside their terms of reference. The influence of this particular factor will become clear when we study the problem of within company departmental performance to which we shall return later in this chapter.

The relations with professional labour are most subtle. Sometimes a professional body will warn its members to be careful in their dealings and in their employment with particular companies, but this is rare. However, there will be important effects on the general ethos of the company and of its approach to decision-making, which will stem from its relations with professional bodies.

The relationship of the organization to its consumers is interesting and sometimes complex. It is not common for a company to sell direct to its consumers. It will generally work through its own customers, that is wholesalers and retailers. For example, most nylon fibres which are spun in this country are sold to manufacturers who are going to make up the product and market it themselves to wholesalers and retailers. Hence advertising of nylon is aimed at the ultimate consumer but in a rather delicate way so that those who lie between the nylon manufacturer and the consumer, namely the manufacturers and customers involved in making up, will not feel that they are being attacked by being forced to use nylon rather than some other product. Much of the advertising that a company carries out may be aimed at these intermediate bodies such as wholesalers and retailers rather than at the ultimate consumer of the product, and there is an interesting and subtle relationship which exists between the company, the customer and the consumer.

The other two forms of relationship are those which exist between the company and the suppliers and rival companies. Companies will create, over a period of years, relationships with particular suppliers and it need not necessarily be the case that the company will buy from the cheapest supplier. The product quality, requirements of meeting delivery dates are as important as the price at which material is bought and, of course, the company itself is only one part of a chain. To its supplier it is an end point whereas to it, the supplier is a beginning point.

Relations with rival companies are not always straightforward. There is not generally a condition of war on all fronts with all rival firms. There will be explicit alliances or even implicit unspoken alliances existing between an organization and its rivals. Sometimes, for example, rival companies will combine to remove uncertainty from certain points of the operation, either by operating joint buying schemes or by exchanging information regarding sources of raw materials, by exchanging market forecasting data, operating joint pressure groups on government or engaging in combined advertising to increase the total market for which they are aiming.

These relationships are expressed schematically in Figure 3.

Pressures on the individual

The executive within the organization exists not only to serve the organization, but also, of course, he is primarily concerned with serving himself. The mindless, grey flannel-suited automaton existing only to serve the corporation

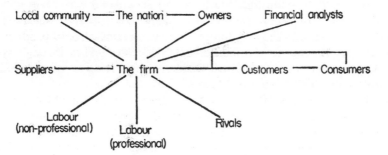

Figure 3. The industrial firm and its pressures

is more a figment of fiction than a reality. Hence when we study the decision-maker we are serving, we have to look at him in two lights. We have first to look at him as simply an employee of the company and also as someone who is concerned with enabling the company to achieve its objectives. Most executives will try honestly and honourably to achieve such an attainment of objectives (when they know what they are), but nevertheless there are other pressures which act on him which may lead him from time to time to work in ways which run counter to organizational well-being. Sometimes this is inevitable in the criteria which the organization imposes on him (and we shall come to such criteria shortly). Most executives are concerned with making their career within the company where they are working. They may not feel that they are going to work in that particular company or organization all their lives and indeed as management becomes more professionalized it may well be that mobility of managers will increase. Professional skills are transferable skills, unless the profession is an effective monopoly such as mining engineering or the army. Nevertheless it is still generally the case that within the time period or horizon which is bounded by an operational research study the executive will be conscious that he will be remaining with the company. Hence we have to look more closely at the relationship of the executive with his parent company.

Like all of us, the executive is a human being who will be concerned with perhaps four main factors (in a later chapter when we consider organizational objectives we will see how similar these are to the individual's objectives). The first objective will be survival and security. He (probably) does not wish to be fired and is concerned to maintain his position within the organization. He will react against any form of study which is likely to influence his security and his possibilities of survival within the organization. The second features of the pressures acting on the executives are linked, namely income and status. In general, income is likely to be a condition which has to be satisfied rather than maximized. It is rare to meet anyone who operates solely to maximize their income (one might reflect that most people working at all levels, including those possibly who are reading this book, could make more money by changing their job. They do not, and I do not, because there is more to life than income and expenditure). Status is important and executives will react against any form of procedure which is likely to affect their status. This is particularly the case in the installation of new systems of data production or provision, or of some form of automatic decision-making through systems analysis. Most executives are sensitive about their relative status within the organization and will guard it jealously.

All this, of course, is affected by the degree of ambition. Most of us will welcome opportunities to enhance our status, income and security because most of us have some form of ambition. Just as every member of parliament would like to be Prime Minister, so most scientists and executives in organizations would like to be on the Board. This is entirely natural and honourable and it is almost a prerequisite of the growth and advancement of an organization that it should have within it a number of people who are hungry for advancement in this way. Ambition, however, can be a dangerous characteristic and the management scientist has to beware of those whose ambition is such as to try to twist the organization or twist investigations in such a way as to satisfy their ambitions.

The model builder must, therefore, be aware that it is not sufficient for him, in creating a model and in implementing his results, to serve solely the overt organizational objectives. Indeed, as a total organization consists of people, perhaps it is wrong to think in the abstract of any group form of organizational objective which is separate from those of the individuals comprising that group. All those who have been concerned in management science with the problems of implementation will be aware of this. It is summed up perhaps most precisely by Machiavelli[6] in a telling passage: 'It should be borne in mind that there is nothing more difficult to arrange, more doubtful of success and more dangerous to carry through than initiating changes in a state's constitution. The innovator makes enemies of all those who prospered under the old order and only lukewarm suport is coming from those who would prosper under the new. Their support is lukewarm partly from fear of adversaries who have the existing laws on their side, and partly because men are generally incredulous, never really trusting new things, unless they have tested them by experience. In consequence, whenever those who oppose the changes can do so, they attack vigorously and the defence made by the others is only lukewarm so both the innovator and his friend are endangered together.'

Objectives, goals and criteria

We have so far introduced some terms and used them imprecisely. The terms should now be defined more explicitly. These are the concepts of objectives, goals and criteria. There will be many different ways of defining such terms, but for the sake of consistency within this book, we shall use the terms in the following way.

By objectives we mean a long term state towards which we hope the organization is proceeding. Such objectives may be unobtainable but nevertheless they are there as the ultimate towards which one is proceeding and are yardsticks against which decisions can be tested. It is tempting for such formulations of objectives to be couched in innocuous high-sounding terms, which in the event do not mean very much. For example, one might state that one requires high employee morale; but unless at the same time a measure is provided which defines what is meant by employee morale, then such a statement is interesting, but not a very good determinant for day-to-day decision-making. We need, therefore, an ultimate long term state of affairs which is stated wherever possible in measurable form or which incorporates units of measurement.

The second statement is that of goals. Goals are measured states in which we want the organization to be, at or during a specific period of time. The goals, therefore, when stated this way are directly related to the statement of the objectives, and it must be shown, for example, that the provision of resources necessary to achieve these goals at these periods of time is feasible and that the goals lie on a logical path towards the objectives.

This statement of objectives and goals corresponds to that of Ackoff. To these we would add one further, namely current criteria of performance. These are those measures which we use as of now to check on the progress of the organization towards its goal. In some cases, objectives, goals and criteria are derived and defined by different parts of an organization without reference to each other and in these cases an organization can develop some form of schizophrenia or exhibit collective neurotic tendencies. Also it is possible for objectives, goals or criteria to conflict within themselves. Sets of criteria of performance, for example, or of goals which seem logical for different parts of an organization may not combine together in a logical manner. An example of this will be introduced at the end of this chapter.

As can be seen from the above this distinction elucidates the distinction between strategy and tactics. Just as objectives, goals and criteria are essentially relative terms, so are strategy and tactics. There is a dangerous tendency to assume that strategy is what one is doing oneself and tactics is what other people are doing. Indeed the term strategy is sometimes used in an essentially tactical way, as in game theory strategies which are micro-tactical choices. Strategy, as Ackoff has described it, is concerned with the long term, whereas tactics are concerned with short term. Strategy will be concerned with the whole of the organization and tactics with part of the organization. The time period of the consequences of strategic decisions will be much greater than the consequence of tactical decisions and, again, in strategic matters there is less opportunity for changing one's mind than there is in the tactical. These obviously are all relative terms that lead us to see that we can effectively equate corporate, strategic and long term when contemplating different forms of planning. (Reference should be made to Ackoff[7] for a fuller and more complete discussion of these points.)

Self-generated conflict

The way in which the large organization is organized has traditionally been to cut the management job down to size. This has been inevitable as the task of the top executive is now too great and complex for it to be discharged satisfactorily or effectively by one man. Hence in a typical manufacturing company one will divide the total tasks into those of purchasing, production, marketing, personnel and finance, amongst others. In addition, where a company operates a number of plants or is in a number of locations, it may well duplicate some of the above functions. At every level one seeks to give one's subordinates tasks which are fully worthy of them, yet which lie within their competence. Since in general a man who has n people reporting to him does not have a brain or memory n times as large as each of these individuals, this superior being will have to be able to extract and condense what his subordinates are doing and to check on the significant features of their tasks. This leads to the derivation of performance criteria by which these separate functions are judged. One of the difficulties is that criteria of performance which are natural and logical when applied within a function do not necessarily match and cohere across functions. Some of the more usual criteria of performance which are used to judge the effectiveness of control of organizations may be found in the following list.

Purchasing

> Raw material costs.
> Raw material quality.
> Raw material stocks.
> Comparison of costs with main competitor(s).
> Comparison of costs with best possible or with average of costs.

Production

> Cost per unit produced.
> Percentage of orders produced on time.
> Percentage of capacity used.
> In-process stocks.
> Overtime worked.
> Accident rate.
> Production per employee.
> Production as function of labour costs.
> Added value per employee.

Marketing

> Volume sold.

Contribution to profits of what is sold.
Finished goods stocks.
Share of market.
Sales per salesman.
Sales as product of stocks.
Deliveries on time/order delays.
Lost orders.
Customer satisfaction.
Customer loyalty.

Personnel

Dispute rates.
Labour turnover.
Absenteeism.
Training costs.
Sickness.
Accidents.

Finance

Return on assets.
Earnings per share.
Total profits.
Profitability compared with main competitors.
Shareholders return.
P/E ratio.

One of the conclusions which can stem from the derivation of such criteria is the possibility of conflict within the organization. Let us take some of the relations which exist between different parts of an organization. If production is judged, amongst other things, by its long term cost of production per unit produced and if marketing, as is usually the case, is judged by the total volume sold, rather than by the contribution to profits of what is sold, then production will require long continuous runs of the same product, while marketing will require a profusion of products of great variety available at every point of sale. Marketing may, in addition, accept changes in the specification or delivery date of a product without reference to or consideration of the impact these changes are likely to have on the production process and on production costs. Hence there is in most organizations a continuing discussion between production and marketing.

Purchasing may be judged by the cost of raw material, irrespective of the impact that this raw material has on the production process. Hence the quality of raw material purchased may not appear in a quantitative form in the performance criteria, and yet it may well affect the performance of both purchasing and production. Finished goods stocks, in-process stocks and raw material stocks will all be subject to attack by the financial controllers since one of their criteria is the return on the assets of the company. In particular, at times of recession, production may manufacture for stock in order to retain skilled workers, whereas it is exactly at this time that finance may want to cut stocks in order to keep up the return on the assets.

Personnel may be judged by criteria such as dispute rates, labour turnover and training costs and hence will be concerned with methods of payment of workers irrespective of the effect these methods of payment and methods of working may have on the production cost. Hence, as can be seen, the interfaces between the different functions of an organization are rich sources of conflict and these themselves can be rich sources of investigation.

Conflict between different departments is not the only way in which the interface can be expressed. Sometimes the logic of a situation is such as to enforce an instability in the ultimate decisions which are taken. Such instability can exist even when conflict is absent. For example, suppose we have a situation in which the marketing department is formulating an estimate of sales in terms of the price at which they are going to charge for the goods. (This example is derived from Ackoff[7]). The price/sales relationship will be of the usual type as shown Figure 4.

If the marketing department criterion is its total volume of sales, then it will wish to have a quantity of goods ordered which will be sufficient to meet sales and they will not wish to run out of stock. In Figure 4 marketing may have one price sales relationship which is a more optimistic one than that which is used

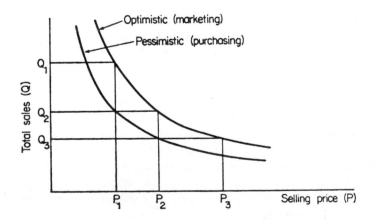

Figure 4. Feedback in marketing-purchasing interface

by purchasing. Now, therefore, if the purchasing officer is judged by the excess of stock, we will then have an unstable situation. For example, if the marketing director selects P_1 as his selling price, he will then forecast the total sales as Q_1. The purchasing manager knows that the marketing manager is optimistic, and hence he will take the P_1 and from his own 'realistic curve' estimate a lower quantity of sales Q_2. In his turn the marketing manager, observing that the quantity of goods ordered is less than he anticipated being sold, will then adjust his price upwards to the price P_2. In turn the purchasing manager will order a still lower quantity, Q_3. As can be seen in this very simple and highly stylized situation, the ultimate is that the goods are priced at infinity and zero are sold. This is an example of a positive feedback situation which can occur in the basic logic of decision-making.[8] When we observe this retrogression to an extreme it can be taken as an indication that such a feedback loop may be operative. In the next chapter, we suggest a simple twofold classification of models. One of these will be those which incorporate feedback within the logic (and the above situation is a typical example of one such model).

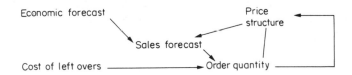

Figure 4a. Feedback loop in marketing-purchasing interface

Conflict in a simple linear programming case

Consider a situation where the finished production of four primary plants is transported to three other secondary plants at which it forms the raw material input. The manufacturing costs, x, at each of the four plants consist of the usual fixed and variable elements and the constraints on the amount produced, p, are:

$$\begin{aligned}
\text{Plant A:} \; x &= 100 + 20p & 30 < p < 70 \\
\text{B:} \; x &= 80 + 30p & 20 < p < 50 \\
\text{C:} \; x &= 70 + 40p & 50 < p < 100 \\
\text{D:} \; x &= 60 + 50p & 30 < p < 80
\end{aligned}$$

For a total production of, say, 250 the allocation p_A, p_B, p_C, p_D which minimises total production cost, subject to the four constraints, is $p_A = 70$, $p_B = 50$, $p_C = 100$, $p_D = 30$, giving a total production cost of 8710.

The production costs and constraints at the secondaries are

$$
\begin{array}{lll}
\text{At E: } & y = 100 + 70p & 60 < p < 120 \\
\text{F: } & y = 250 + 20p & 100 < p < 150 \\
\text{G: } & y = 150 + 50p & 40 < p < 60
\end{array}
$$

The minimum total production cost allocation at the three plants is 60, 150, 40, respectively, with a total of 9700.

Finally, consider now the transport costs (in £'s per unit) from each of these four primary plants to each of the three secondary plants, E, F, G, say,

	E	F	G
A	15	20	35
B	40	35	10
C	10	60	25
D	30	20	40

If the amounts produced, P_A, P_B, P_C, P_D are, respectively, 70, 50, 100, 30 and the amounts consumed, P_E, P_F, P_G are, respectively, 60, 150, 40, then the minimal transport allocation is:

	E	F	G	
A	0	70	0	(70)
B	0	50	0	(50)
C	60	0	40	(100)
D	0	30	0	(30)
	(60)	(150)	(40)	

giving a transport cost of 5350. Hence, with the three separate optimal policies, the total cost is 8710 + 9700 + 5350 = 23,750.

However, if we treat the *whole* problem rather than three separate parts we set the amounts to be produced at A, B, C, D,; the amounts to be consumed at E, F, G; and the transport allocation so that we obtain an *overall* minimum pf production cost + transport cost + production cost.

In this case the production is

$$
\begin{array}{ll}
P_A = 70 & \text{Cost} = 1500 \\
P_B = 50 & \text{Cost} = 1580 \\
P_C = 60 & \text{Cost} = 2470 \\
P_D = 70 & \text{Cost} = 3560
\end{array}
$$

Total production cost = 9110 (compared with 8710)

The consumption is

$$P_E = 60 \qquad \text{Cost} = 4300$$
$$P_F = 150 \qquad \text{Cost} = 3250$$
$$P_G = 40 \qquad \text{Cost} = 2150$$

Total = 9700 as before.

The minimum transport cost for these amounts is

	E	F	G	
A	0	70	0	(70)
B	0	10	40	(50)
C	60	0	0	(60)
D	0	70	0	(70)
	(60)	(150)	(40)	

with a cost of 4150, giving a total cost of 9110 + 9700 + 4150 = 22960, a reduction of 800 from the solution of the three separate optima.

In deriving performance criteria we have to be careful to ensure that criteria which are applied to separate parts of an organization will continue to make sense when applied to the totality. If we have a parameter (or a criterion of performance) which, when applied to separate parts, is λ_i for each of the n parts and is λ when applied to the whole then it is *not* necessary that

$$\text{if } \frac{d\lambda_i}{dt} > 0 \text{ for all } i$$

$$\text{then } \frac{d\lambda}{dt} > 0.$$

This will be no surprise to the cricket lovers who will remember the sad examples of bowlers A and B. Before they each went into a match they had the same bowling average:

Bowler A — 10 wickets for 200 runs; average 20 runs per wicket
Bowler B — 1 wicket for 20 runs; average 20 runs per wicket

In the match Bowler A performed better than Bowler B, for A took one wicket for 140 runs and B took no wicket for 10 runs. But the bowling average of A was now *worse* than that of B, for his average is now

$$\frac{340}{11} = 30 \cdot 9$$

and that of B is

$$\frac{30}{1} = 30.$$

There are similar data from real life. For example*, Tables 1 to 6 show the sales of cigarettes achieved by the American Tobacco Company during the 1950s. This was the time which saw the gradual introduction of filter, kingsize and menthol cigarettes in addition to the regular cigarettes which had been the staple product. An examination of the shares of market obtained by the American Tobacco Company in the separate product markets (four in number) compared with the total market show some interesting paradoxes.

As can be seen from Tables 1 to 6, there are a number of years in which the share of market of the Company in each of the separate product groups increased, while at the same time their share of total markets decreased. In addition there are years in which the reverse applied. Consequently, we must be careful not to use what seem to be logical ratios in a too unthinking fashion. If we seek to control the separate parts of an organization by certain criteria of performance, it would not necessarily be the case when those criteria are improving that the total system, as judged by the same criteria, will also be improving.

It cannot be too strongly urged that the derivation of a criterion of performance is complex. Whenever we use a unit of measurement with which to study a particular set of operations we are assuming that the form of the objective function is such that this particular unit is a dominant and significant factor. Often by the act of selecting a unit of measurement we are prejudging a total situation and are forcing ourselves inevitably towards certain conclusions. This perhaps is one of the most serious criticisms which can be made about the treatment of financial and cost data.

There is an interesting commentary here on the difference between descriptive and explanatory checking of data. When the first edition of this book was published there was an error in Table 2. The figure for King size cigarettes in 1957 was printed as 94·3 and not 84·3. An accountant who kindly spotted the error assumed in fact that the 94·3 was correct and that the error was in the total of 407·5, which he thought should have been 417·5. This was the descriptive approach. An explanatory approach would be to observe that the sequence down the Kingsize column would be more credible if the 1957 figure was less than that for 1956 and hence the error must be in that figure and not in the total.

The cigarette data illustrate the important fact that measurement is not neutral but always incorporates a view of the world. In the light of the example we have to decide in monitoring the progress of the company, whether to use total share of market or sector share of market. But more importantly, both these figures imply the view of the world that the company is only in competition with other cigarette companies. Using these data as 'facts' will

---

*I am indebted to Dr. R. S. Weinberg for these data.

Table 1

	Total industry cigarette sales†	American Tobacco cigarette sales	American share of the market	Tobacco Company net change in share of the market
	(billions of cigarettes)		(per cent)	
1950	361·4	113·0	31·27	—
1951	377·4	121·0	32·06	+0·79
1952	391·7	128·5	32·81	+0·75
1953	391·0	127·8	32·69	—0·12
1954	367·1	123·0	33·51	+0·82
1955	377·8	124·0	32·82	—0·69
1956	388·5	122·3	31·48	—1·34
1957	407·5	119·0	29·20	—2·28
1958	433·5	115·5	26·64	—2·56
1959	460·2	120·6	26·21	—0·43

†Big six manufactures

Table 2

	Industry cigarette sales by product class 1950-1959				
	(billions of cigarettes)				
	Regular	King	Filter	Mentholated	Total
1951	314·7	35·3	2·2	9·2	361·4
1951	315·7	48·0	3·2	10·5	377·4
1952	305·0	70·3	4·9	11·5	391·7
1953	264·8	102·4	12·3	11·5	391·0
1954	215·8	102·0	37·2	12·1	367·1
1955	193·4	97·7	74·0	12·7	377·8
1956	172·4	91·2	108·6	16·3	388·5
1957	154·5	84·3	142·3	26·4	407·5
1958	142·7	86·2	167·5	37·1	433·5
1959	136·8	86·4	185·3	51·7	460·2

Table 3

American Tobacco Company cigarette sales by product class
1950-1959

	(billions of cigarettes)				
	Regular	King	Filter	Mentholated	Total
1950	82·5	30·5	—	—	113·0
1951	79·0	42·0	—	—	121·0
1952	73·5	55·0	—	—	128·5
1953	66·3	61·5	—	—	127·8
1954	58·5	63·0	1·5	—	123·0
1955	57·5	63·0	3·5	—	124·0
1956	55·5	61·4	5·4	—	122·3
1957	51·5	59·4	8·1	—	119·0
1958	47·2	61·5	6·8	—	115·5
1959	44·5	66·2	9·7	0·2	120·6

Table 4

American Tobacco Company share of the market by product class
1950-1959

	(per cent)				
	Regular	King	Filter	Mentholated	Total
1950	26·22	86·40	—	—	31·27
1951	25·02	87·50	—	—	32·06
1952	24·10	78·23	—	—	32·81
1953	25·04	60·06	—	—	32·69
1954	27·11	61·77	4·03	—	33·51
1955	29·73	64·48	4·73	—	32·82
1956	32·19	67·32	4·97	—	31·48
1957	33·33	70·46	5·69	—	29·20
1958	33·08	71·35	4·06	—	26·64
1959	32·53	76·62	5·23	0·39	26·21

Table 5

American Tobacco Company — net change in share of market by product class 1951-1959				
(per cent)				
	Regular	King	Filter	Mentholated	Total
1951	—1·20	+1·10	—	—	+0·79
1952	·—0·092	—9·27	—	—	+0·75
1953	+0·94	—18.17	—	—	—0·12
1954	+2·07	+1·71	+4·03	—	+0·82
1955	+2·62	+2·71	+0·70	—	—0·69
1956	+2·46	+2·84	+0·24	—	—1·34
1957	+1·14	+3·14	+0·72	—	—2·28
1958	—0·25	+0·89	—1·63	—	—2·56
1959	—0·55	+5·27	+1·17	+0·39	—0·43

Table 6

The structure of the cigarette market 1950-1959				
(percentage of total market)				
	Regular	King	Filter	Mentholated	Total
1950	87·08	9·77	0·61	2·54	100·00
1951	83·65	12·72	0·85	2·73	100·00
1952	77·87	17·95	1·24	2·94	100·00
1953	67·72	26·19	3·15	2·94	100·00
1954	58·78	27·79	10·13	3·30	100·00
1955	51·19	25·86	19·59	3·36	100·00
1956	44·38	23·47	27·95	4·20	100·00
1957	37·91	20·69	34·92	6·48	100·00
1958	32·92	19·86	38·64	8·56	100·00
1959	29·73	18·77	40·27	11·23	100·00

ignore the view that cigarettes might be in competition with cigars, pipe smoking, chocolates and sweets or food.

A simpler (but fabricated) further example of criteria, which make sense when applied to a part but make nonsense when applied to the whole, arises with the minimax criterion.

Consider a man who has two people working for him, both of whom are playing a game against nature. They each have two courses of action a or b and c or d, respectively, and nature can be in one of two states X or Y.

The costs are as follows:

		X	Y
For first person:	a	5	2
	b	3	3
For second person:	c	2	5
	d	3	3

Under minimax, the optimal courses of action are b and d for each person.

But from the view of the person for whom they are both working, the costs are additive:

	X	Y
ac	7	7
ad	8	5
bc	5	8
bd	6	6

Minimax applied to the sum, yields ac, that is the precise opposite of the criterion applied to each separately.

However, a view of the world may also be inbuilt another way. In the 1950's a study was to be made of absenteeism in the coal industry. As a first step lists were made of the mines with the highest absenteeism and of the mines with the highest attendance, with a view to discovering whether there were any obvious environmental reasons. To the surprise of the investigators it was discovered that many mines were on *both* lists, that is according to published statistics they simultaneously suffered high absenteeism and enjoyed high attendance. Further analysis showed the reason. Absenteeism was defined as the proportion of shifts worked Monday to Friday. Attendance was deduced from equivalent manshifts over the seven days of the week. Mines with high 5-day absenteeism have to bring in extra workers on Saturday and Sunday to make up the work.

Moreover weekend working is at double pay. Any study separately of attendance or absenteeism would have proceeded on the basis of what appeared reasonable data. It was only when they were brought into conjunction that it was realised that a choice had to be made.

3 Cause-Effect Structures

'The people that doth not understand shall fall'

Hosea

Classification of variables

It will now be useful to outline what is meant by some of the standard terms used in model building and to illustrate these by a specific example.

In every decision-making situation there will be variables which have to be estimated or manipulated. Some of these variables will be external to the decision-maker's problem and can be treated as states of nature. These environmental variables may appear to be essentially uncontrollable, but controllability is relative. It may be possible to forecast what these uncontrollable variables will be and sometimes they are under control of a malevolent opponent. We shall return to the particular case of variables controllable by an opponent in a later chapter on competitive modelling. In the non-competitive situations, however, we have the straight two-fold classification between the uncontrollable variables which are mainly environmental and the decision variables which are those which lie within the control of the decision-maker. To a certain extent of course the decision or controllable variables will not necessarily encompass the total of all the decisions undertaken within an organization. For example, a manager at a given level may be forced to treat decisions taken by executives two levels above him as being uncontrollable. Equally, it is not the case that all those in an inferior position to a given manager will necessarily do what he says. The extent of control downwards in an organization is probably as tenuous as the extent of influence upwards and, in analysying the variables which affect the outcome of a decision, we may have to treat decisions taken by inferiors as being as uncontrollable as the states of nature. The consequence of this is that in any study of the variables which impinge on a decision we must have a firm understanding of and a feeling for the management ethos, tradition and discipline. In many cases it is difficult, if not impossible, to treat variables in a clear division between controllable and uncontrollable. There will inevitably be areas of overlap. Nevertheless, some form of ranking of variables along a spectrum of controllability is essential as a first stage of decision analysis.

The model is the subject of this book. Essentially a model is an attempt to extract from the richness of a real situation and so to formulate a concept which can be manipulated and controlled. Hence every model has at its heart a many-one transformation in which the many variables of the real situation are classified and either ignored, treated in groups or treated singly. In addition these variables are linked by a basic logic. It is one of the tasks of model building to try to understand the real situation and to formulate in a hypothetical form the logical patterns of causes and effect which link together the controllable and the uncontrollable variables.

As will be seen, two of the main techniques used in model formulation and solution will be those of mathematics and of statistics. It will be noted that, on the whole, statistical methods are used to test the significance of the model (that is its goodness of fit) and to forecast the uncontrollable variables. In general, mathematical techniques are used in the solution of objective functions. Such a classification is not, of course, exclusive or exhaustive, but it is a good working rule which helps to put into perspective the subject of statistics in relation to operational research. As can be seen there is no equivalence, or one-to-one mapping, between the statistical method and the operational research model-building method.

Generalized structure

The model draws together some of the concepts so far discussed:

(a) Controllable variables
(b) Uncontrollable variables
(c) Objective functions
(d) Constraints

The first stage is to formulate, however tentatively, some idea of the objectives and goals. The second is to suggest, on the basis of an understanding of the decision maker's task, the boundaries to his sphere of concern. This will indicate the variables which affect his task, some of these variables being controllable and others uncontrollable. The logical connections in qualitative form from these variables of entry into his sphere of concern, to the objectives and goals are then suggested, taking account of the constraints, legal, social, economic, ethical under which the systems must operate; for example:

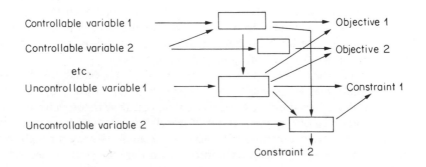

Within this schema it can be seen that entry nodes correspond with the controllable and uncontrollable variables and terminal nodes with objectives and constraints. But what of the nodes which contain both entry and exit arrows? These identify those parts of the system where analysis is necessary, and which also in its turn identifies the data which must be made available.

Now clearly the inputs to and outputs from these nodes must be commensurable otherwise the analysis at the node is impossible. Hence, where there are incommensurables involved we may be forced to separate models for each objective function. This is not inevitable, as a moment's thought will show, but it is a possibility that has to be borne in mind.

In the following example there are different measures involved, for example lecture room loading and research output, but they can be accommodated within one diagram.

An example of structure

A specific example will be helpful and will show the way in which a cause-effect hypothesis can be built into a model. Consider the question of applications from prospective undergraduates to gain a university place. Let us assume that each student will apply to up to six courses at different universities. Each university will take up references for the students and may interview some of them. As a result of this the student will receive from each of the universities concerned, either a firm unconditional offer of a place, a conditional offer which states the 'A' level grades he must obtain in the three subjects for entry, or, finally, he may be rejected. After receiving these six replies each student can then hold one as a firm acceptance and one as a provisional acceptance. If he obtains the conditions laid down in the offer he accepted on a firm basis, then he is obliged to take the course in question. On the other hand he is under no obligation to accept a course which he accepts provisionally. It can be seen that university departments face a daunting task. They have to put out sufficient offers to ensure that on the first day of term the right number of students arrive to take their courses. There are penalty costs which a university department will suffer from errors which it makes in this process. If too many students are received then this causes congestion which may, in the case of science subjects with limited laboratory space, even become catastrophic. On the other hand if too few students arrive to take the course then the department itself will be under pressure from other departments in the university to yield resources which have been earmarked for it against this postential demand. Consequently this situation is fraught with danger.

Consider now the students who arrive on Day One. Let us assume that within the department concerned they can take six different courses out of twelve offered. At the end of the first year, those who continue through to the second year may take three further courses out of the six topics which were taken in the first year. In the third year those who were successful in moving through to their finals will take one subject out of the three which were taken in the second year.

In the Science Faculty these students will make demands upon the laboratory space available and we can assume that the space which they need is proportional to the number of students. The students will make demands on lecture facilities, which are expressed partly in terms of human facilities such as lecturers, and partly in terms of demands made on lecture rooms both by size and by number. In a university which operates a tutorial system there will, in addition, be demands made both on staff and on physical facilities for tutorial rooms which will be *pro rata* to the number of students. There will in addition be the flow-through of third year students into post graduate subjects and these will have certain time lags within the system.

Hence we see that the resources which are available to meet the demands of students are two types, the human and the physical. The human will comprise lecturers, research assistants and technicians while the physical type will comprise lecture rooms, staff rooms, tutorial rooms, laboratories and libraries.

The basic logic of this total system is structured in Figure 5. As can be seen from the diagram there are a number of boxes of entry to this total system and these entry boxes correspond with the controllable and uncontrollable variables which are operating on the system.

It may be noticed that there are also a number of terminal boxes. These correspond with objective functions and constraints. For example, lecture room loading is a constraint under which the system will operate, whereas the number of post graduates emerging from the department each year can be regarded as one of the objectives of the system.

It is difficult to define the objectives of a university department. At one level we have the teaching function which leads towards the educational process being expressed in terms of the graduate output. On another level we have the research of the members of faculty. It is often thought that the two main functions of a university are teaching and research but the real function of a university is intellectual creativity. If this is the case, the reason for having students in the system at all is obscure but perhaps such a requirement can be put within the general heading of 'Research Output'.

As can be seen from the above problem, the variables under which the system operates are as follows: *controllable variables*—the amount of laboratory space available, the number of technicians available, the number of faculty by subject, the number of lecture rooms, number and type of offers made; *uncontrollable variables*—the number of students applying, the number and type of acceptances, the choices of subjects. The *constraints*, which appear as terminal boxes, are lecture room loading, faculty loading, tutorial and faculty rooms, and the *objectives* are the research output, the number of graduates emerging and the number of post graduates emerging.

It can also be seen that what is controlled and uncontrolled depends on the viewpoint and also our own confidence of controllability. The number of students applying can, for example, be influenced by changes in course content. But such a change, and knowledge of its probabilistic consequence, may be beyond the time horizon of the particular present decision being

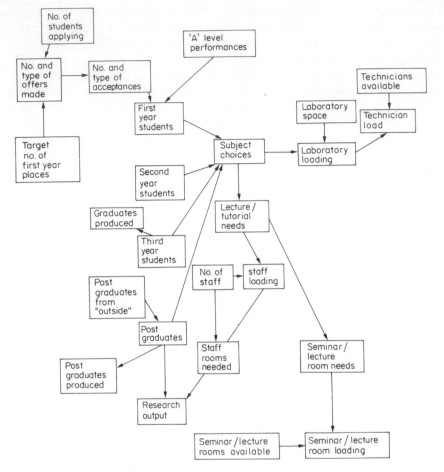

Figure 5. Student applications model

considered. We must always guard against our model being too small, of it failing to take account of the larger system (in the present case should the model cover the system of the whole university, the system of all universities, the system of adult education?). We must guard, in a word, against sub-optimization, while remembering that the boundary must be put somewhere, as only God optimizes.

We have now formulated a total model for the above situation. We must however be careful to understand that we do not delay formulating a logical system until we have received the total information about it. In any study we receive information sequentially. At every stage of this sequence we adapt our ideas and change the form of the model. It is rather as though with the first information we start with a very simple basic structure and everything else we learn tends to be added to this basic structure. Hence it may be the case that the form of the model which we derive is a function of the order in which we have received information by which we have learnt about the total system. De Bono gives an example in which the reader is invited to add a series of given shapes together so that at each stage the resulting shape can be described in words. The last piece in the series cannot be added to produce a describable shape. However, if the whole group is broken down and reassembled, they can be formed into a square. In a similar manner, when any model is constructed we should ask whether it would have been significantly different had our progressive understanding and data availability gone through a different sequence.

4 Classification of Models

'The sheep on the right and goats on the left'
St. Matthew

Why classify?

Many research workers have formulated methods of classifying models. Before presenting some of the better known examples it is useful to ask the question why we want to classify these models anyway. Man seems to be a classifying animal and we are always tempted to put everything we observe into a category. The usefulness of this will be a function of the other members of the same category, for we hope that members of the same category will exhibit characteristics which are shared in common against the phenomena we are interested in. Hence we are concerned with forms of classification which will hasten our understanding of structure and hasten the process of solving the model. In some cases, forms of model classification have been proposed which are purely technique-oriented. This is obviously helpful in that once one knows the technique category one is dealing with, then it is fairly simple to know the methods of approach and to be able to appeal to previous work. However, generally in model solution the technique by which the problem is to be solved is the last thing which one understands, and to classify models according to techniques used is the ultimate putting of the cart before the horse. We therefore reject methods of classification which are purely technique-oriented. These are entirely unhelpful.

Seven basic structures

An early method of classification was that devised by Ackoff and Rivett.[9] They made the distinction between the form and content of the problem and concentrated on the purely tactical level. By 'content' was meant the surface flesh of complexity in which the problem appeared. Hence there are certain problems with the content of steel-making, of confectionery, of mining, of transport, of service and so on. On the other hand, behind this surface flesh of complexity will lie a form which shows the structural relationship of some of the variables. Problems can arise in different contexts, which will have the same form. Ackoff and Rivett make the point, quite firmly, that their classification is neither exhaustive nor complete. Indeed the more strategic the type of problem the greater is the likelihood of more than one model being needed, and yet it is a useful approach to this problem. They suggest seven main forms of problem, which we shall now take in turn. (It is to be regretted that this sevenfold classification was subsequently embraced with so much enthusiasm as to encourage others to suggest, and even dogmatically to state, such things as 'all management problems are of one of the seven types'. This is the most arrant nonsense.)

1. *Queuing problems*

Although at first sight this is a technique classification, any knowledge of the subject will lead to the conclusion that queuing theory is hardly an applicable theory in the sense of being useful in solving anything, and hence to classify problems as queuing problems is not to cling to a technique. In all queuing problems there is a relationship between a server and the served, and typical in this relationship is the fact that the greater the efficiency with which the service operation is carried out (if measured in terms of the amount of time the service operation is being productive) the less efficient will be the activity of the served.

The basic structure of a queuing problem is the 'in, service, out' as seen in Figure 6. Items arriving for service will wait until the service point is unoccupied when one of them will proceed in to be served.

An everyday example of queuing is a barber's shop. In this customers wait in a common queue until the next barber is available. A more complex queue is at a post office or a bank where the customer on entry has to commit himself to a particular service point, although he can transfer from one queue to another.

The basic structure is:

Figure 6. Basic structure of queuing

In all queuing problems there is a conflict between the server and the served. The former wants high productivity at the service point; this means that the service point should be operating continuously. But this can only be achieved at the expense of the served; the object of the served is to move into service immediately and this can only be done if the service point is empty when he arrives. Consequently, unless the server pays some form of compensation to the served in terms of the time he spends in the system, or vice versa, there is no single objective function that can be applied to the system as a whole.

For a barber's shop, a cause effect structure could be:

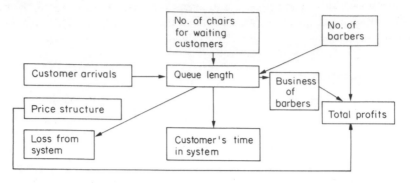

Figure 7

There are two terminal boxes, corresponding to these objectives. We note that if the business of the barbers increases, this can only stem from a longer queue. It seems paradoxical that the customer's time in the system can only decrease if the productivity of the barbers *decreases*. This truth is not always recognised by those who operate (or plan) service facilities. In particular we may consider the queuing problem of an engineering job shop which deals with (randomly arriving) orders. If the capacity of the shop matches the average demand, the length of work backlog will be unstable and overtime will be commonplace.

2. *Inventory problems*

In some curious way inventory has assumed the characteristic of immorality, in the sense that inventory is regarded as unproductive, idle resources. Inventory is something much more positive and productive than this.

An inventory problem arises wherever there is a need to uncouple fluctuations in supply from fluctuations in demand. If there is a direct coupling between supplier and supplied then the random nature of the demand made by the supplied will be such as to cause grave embarrassment to the production processes of the supplier. This embarrassment is reflected back to the supplied in a time lag before he receives what he has ordered. Consequently we use an inventory as a way of uncoupling the system. Inventory therefore is a smoothing device and, in-process, inventory is as productive as any other machine on the production line. As with other machines, inventories can have too great a capacity, in which case there will be idle resources. On the other hand an inventory 'machine' can have too small a capacity and this will have the same effect as a small capacity machine on a production line. If inventories are too low, this will be reflected on the production line by a failure to smooth out the irregularities in supply and demand, and production will be subject to delays and idle time. The problem of inventory is the problem of manipulating this stock so that the combination of the cost of manipulating the stock against that of failing to meet the demand will be minimized. In schematic form this is shown in Figure 8.

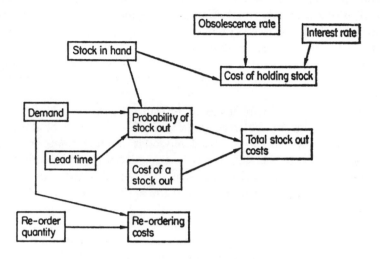

Figure 8. Structure of inventory

An interesting example of inventory is that of the cash held in tills at branch banks. Some branches are net receivers of cash, while others are net payers and there are, of course, day-of-the-week and day-of-the-month effects. Money in the tills is idle money, it does not even count as an eligible liquid reserve against which cash can be lent. With high interest rates it is particularly expensive. On the other hand, there are obvious costs involved in running out of cash. A study of the balance sheets of the clearing banks will show that notwithstanding inflation there has been a run down of hundreds of millions of pounds of cash in tills from the application of simple probability laws.

Where inventories represent an investment (as they always do) there may be an overlap with allocation problems, as will be seen in the section which follows.

There is an important point to be made about cost data used in inventory problems. The costs involved are

(a) Stockholding costs.
(b) Re-ordering (or set-up) costs.
(c) Outage costs.

It will be seen that all of these are opportunity costs (see Chapter 5). Such costs are gossamer things, difficult to nail down and all contain an element of horse trading in their derivation. The analyst has to be careful, as in horse trading, not to take the first cost that is offered to him by the accountant.

3. *Allocation problems*

Allocation problems arise whenever there is a set of resources which can be set against different demands which may be made on them. The allocation of a particular group of resources to a particular activity will make a contribution towards the achievement of an objective, and the concern in these problems is to devise the way in which the resources should be split against the tasks, so that the total achievement of the objective is maximized (or minimized, as the case may be).

In general, allocation problems are deterministic in form and it is often the case that the relationship between the degree of attainment of the objective and the extent of resources which are deployed is of a linear nature. When this is the case the methods of linear programming will apply. The simplest form of linearity is in the structurally simplest type of allocation problem. For example, in mining there is the problem of the optimal allocation of a group of equipment to a set of coal faces. Each equipment can only be put on one face and each face can only be worked by one equipment. Each equipment-face combination will demand requirements of skilled manpower and will yield a total amount of coal with a given size distribution. Linear programming can be used to determine an optimal allocation of loaders to faces. Such a solution may be sensible to the estimates of manpower and coal yield and sensitivity analysis is essential. It might be better to utilise an allocation that was non-

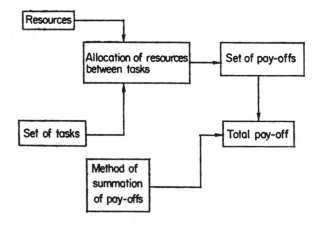

Figure 9. Structure of allocation

optimal but nevertheless was still fairly good even with errors in the input data, that is, one that was robust.

In some cases problems of inventory and competition (see Chapter 9) are approached by means of an allocation structure. For example, it is sometimes the case that probabilistic problems can be turned into deterministic allocation problems by dealing with expectations of return rather than probability distributions. An example of this is in the replenishment of finished goods inventory. Consider a textile plant which is producing printed cloth which has a seasonal life only. Any line which has goods left on hand at the end of a season is sold at a distress price. Orders have to be met immediately from stock and week by week during the season the production (printing) capacity is allocated between the various alternative lines. How should this be done? Clearly the information (that is, in terms of Figure 1, the state of the system) which is relevant is

(a) The week.
(b) The sales so far achieved, line by line.
(c) Current stock on hand, line by line.
(d) The contribution to profit of a unit of sales, line by line.
(e) The loss of a distress sale, line by line.

An obvious approach is to estimate for each line the probability that a further unit of production will be sold by the end of the season, bearing in mind any stocks already on hand. From this, (d) and (e) will now yield the expected profit of a further unit of any one line. The first unit to be scheduled into production will be that with the largest expectation. A second unit of this line (with a lower probability of sale and hence a lower expected profit) can then be compared with a first unit of each of the others and once again the most profitable single one selected. In this way the total capacity can be booked on a daily, or weekly, basis so as to maximise the expected value of the increased inventory and the objective function is then this expectation.

4. Scheduling and routing

These problems arise in deciding the way in which an agreed total task should be approached and controlled. The well-known methods of critical path analysis treat the problem of scheduling through a network and enable the control process to be continuously concentrated on those aspects of the total task which are critical in determining the most efficient way of attaining the overall objective. As an example of the way in which two problems of different content can have the same form, let us take the classical travelling salesman problem and compare it with the machine scheduling problem. In the first case we have to travel between a set of destinations in such a way as to visit them all once only and to minimize the total journey time. In the second case we have the problem of ordering a flow of tasks through a machine where there is a down time between each task which is a function of the preceding and following task. In this case we have to select the order of work so as to minimize the total down time in the operation. These are the same problems in form, although their content differs. In schematic form this is shown in Figure 10(a) and (b).

There are standard algorithms available for such problems. An interesting and important variant in the travelling salesman problem is where there is a particular value in visiting a given destination at a particular time. For example, in the cash in bank tills example (p. 45) the full statement of the problem would include the transport of cash by a bullion van. In this case there is a value attached to visiting a branch at a particular time measured by the time since the last visit and the time to the next visit, since these two periods will affect the amount of cash being held, and the standard algorithms, which assume all visits are of equal value, will not apply.

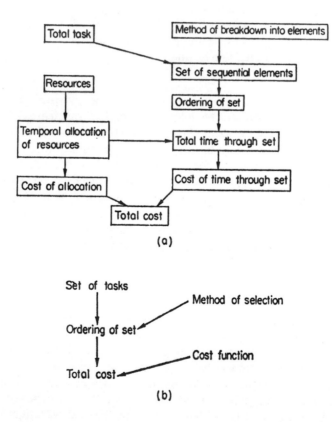

(a)

(b)

Figure 10 (a) & (b). Structure of scheduling

5. *Replacement and maintenance*

The title accurately describes the structure. Units in a system are subject to deterioration in performance and random failure, both as a function of time. Maintenance will affect the performance and the probability of failure. Replacement can either be cyclical or can wait upon failure. The objective is to minimize total expected cost.

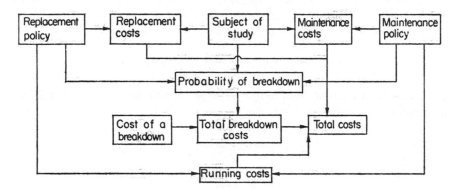

Figure 11. Structure of replacement and maintenance

6. *Search problems*

In problems of search we are engaged in using resources so as to track down a missing target. This will happen in the effort devoted to research and development; it can happen in checking data for errors and it stems from the original work on submarine hunting which gives the problem field its title. This is shown in schematic form in Figure 12.

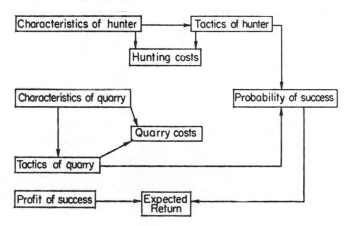

Figure 12. Structure of search

7. *Competition*

Competitive problems are fundamentally different from all the preceding six in that the basic assumption in the earlier classifications is that the variables of nature do not consciously react against the decision-maker in the light of the controllable variables which he selects. In other words, the uncontrollable variables act independently of the selection of controllable variables. In competitive problems there is a third class of variable, namely those which are controlled by an opponent. Competitive problems dichotomize into two classes. There are those in which the response of the opponent to the selection of the controllable variables is so sluggish that he may be regarded as part of nature.

On the other hand there are those situations where the response of a competitor is very rapid and, in a special case, simultaneous. We shall return to the problems of model building in competitive situations more specifically in Chapter 9.

Ackoff-Sasieni classification

The above is an approach to classification of model building which, as can be seen, is largely separated from any particular technique. As has been mentioned, queuing theory has but little relationship to the solution of problems with the form of queuing. Inventory control theory is devised specifically for inventory problems although it may often be the case that the form of technique approach used in inventory problems is more likely to be that of simultation, particularly where the much more complex problems of inventory and production control in a job shop are concerned. Allocation will often be approached by an appeal to mathematical programming and in scheduling and routing the methods of network analysis can be used. Such theory has no body of theory specifically attached to it and tends to be approached by *ad hoc* methodology. In competitive problems there are, as we shall see, a variety of technical approaches with varying degrees of usefulness. A survey of the literature shows that one of the difficulties facing the research-worker on competitive problems is that the literature itself is not self-critical and, unfortunately, the solutions proposed to problems in competition tend to be marketed as though they were consumer products.

Another form of classification is that proposed by Ackoff and Sasieni.[10] This has the interesting approach of classifying problems according to the difficulty of formulating the structure. It is not immediately apparent to this classification will lead to more rapid solutions of problems or, more important, more rapid recognition of the important questions to be asked in approaching these problems. However, it is an interesting method which we now present.

1. *The newsboy problem*

This is an archetype of those problems in which the logical structure is simple and transparent enough to be solved by an inspection or discussion. In the particular case of the newsboy problem the newsboy has to decide how many newspapers to carry in stock. There is a probability distribution of demand for his sales in any day, there is a contribution to profit of every newspaper which he sells and there is a contribution to loss of newspapers with which he is left at the end of the day. The problem is to select the right order quantity in such a way as to maximize the difference between the expected profit and expected loss. As can be seen, this has a straightforward structure; the relationship between the variables involved is clear and can be structured in terms of a logical flow chart as shown in Figure 13.

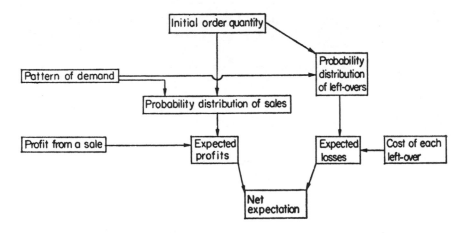

Figure 13. The newsboy problem

The textile finished goods inventory problem referred to on page 47 in terms of maximising the added value of inventory is also an example of the newsboy problem.

2.

In the second category the structure of the problem is apparent but the way in which to represent it symbolically is not clear. In many cases it is possible to solve such problems by the use of an analogy or an iconic model. For example, suppose we have a product which has a known demand at a number of towns and we wish to determine the optimum location of a warehouse from which these demands will be set. The total transport cost is defined as the product of the amount carried from the warhouse to each of the destinations in turn, multiplied by the actual tonnage on each of these routes. The method of solving this analytically is not trivial, but a rapid solution can be obtained as follows. If we represent each of the towns by their appropriate position on a map, we bore a hole at each town in the map and suspend weights on a string through each of these holes. The weight at each hole is proportional to the demand at that particular location. These strings are then joined together and the equilibrium point for the knot is determined. This equilibrium point corresponds with the minimum transport location. For equilibrium

$$\sum W_i \cos \alpha_i = o \tag{1}$$

$$\sum W_i \sin \alpha_i = o \tag{2}$$

where

$$\cos \alpha_i = \frac{x_i - X}{[(x_i - X)^2 + (y_i - Y)^2]^{\frac{1}{2}}} \tag{3}$$

and

$$\sin \alpha_i = \frac{y_i - Y}{[(x_i - X)^2 + (y_i - Y)^2]^{\frac{1}{2}}} \tag{4}$$

Substituting (3) and (4) in (1) and (2) gives

$$\sum \frac{W_i(x_i - X)}{[(x_i - X)^2 + (y_i - Y)^2]^{\frac{1}{2}}} = o \tag{5}$$

and

$$\sum \frac{W_i(y_i - Y)}{[(x_i - X)^2 + (y_i - Y)^2]^{\frac{1}{2}}} = o \tag{6}$$

But the total transport cost is

$$\sum W_i[(x_i - X)^2 + (y_i - Y)^2]^{\frac{1}{2}}$$

and this is minimized for (X, Y) when (5) and (6) apply.

An interesting result of this is that, of course, the optimum location is not the centre of gravity of points in question. The immediate and apparently paradoxical extension of this is shown in the following diagram where we have three destinations which happen to lie in a straight line. As can be seen if the left-hand destination, A, is moved due westwards (even to infinity) the optimum location of the warehouse will still remain at B.

```
         ←――――― West
        A←              10 miles              →B←1 mile→C

        o ――――――――――――――――――――――――――――――――――― o ――――― o
     (10 tons)                              (10 tons)  (1 ton)
```

3.

The third category is that in which the structure of the problem is not apparent but nevertheless there is the possibility of extracting structure by data analysis. As has been said before, this is one of the most dangerous of the methods of approach. It is dangerous because there is always the temptation for us to see what we are looking for. Hence, although the normal approach to formulating a structure should always be to do this via understanding and explicitly through a formal hypothesis, we shall always in this category be looking for structure to be yielded by data analysis. When a piece of statistical analysis gives a relationship between a number of variables we are greatly tempted to assume that there is a casual relationship. One of the most interesting examples in this area is given by Ackoff[10] and concerns the sales of petrol from petrol stations.

As Ackoff recounts it, this study was carried out for a large oil company which had been interested in the problem of discovering the factors which affected a sale of petrol from stations. It had first of all invited motivational research scientists to study the problem. They carried out depth interviews of motorists which indicated the importance of the gasoline attendants as father figures to the motorist. A second study was then carried out by a group of economists. The economists asked each of the twelve leading marketing experts in the company to list what he thought were the three most important factors in determining petrol sales. Between them the marketeers produced 24 different factors and hence there was little in common between their practical experience. A basic regression model of the following form was formulated.

$$S = a_1x_1 + a_2x_2 + \ldots + a_{24}x_{24}$$

A data analysis was then performed in order to estimate the co-efficients a_i, but when this was done it was seen that petrol sales could not be estimated with any useful accuracy. The research team from the Case Institute of Technology, led by Ackoff, then studied this problem. They observed that all the petrol stations were in urban areas and that part of the assumption of the oil industry was that stations should be located at road junctions. Within the urban network of an American town this meant that the road junctions were all at right angled junctions of four roads. The team observed the number of vehicles which used the petrol station on each of the 16 routes by which cars could proceed in and out of such a junction. From this study it was seen that the overwhelming majority of the petrol sales at a station could be accounted for by the sales to cars on only four of the 16 routes. Figure 14 shows the typical problem and the four routes in question.

Within the terms that we have outlined above, this now gives a descriptive model of the problem. It would certainly avail one, given any new junction at which it is proposed to locate a petrol station, of a very good estimate of the potential sales. It would also enable one to study existing petrol stations from

C

54

which a study could then be made of the divergencies from expectation. However, a descriptive model is never good enough if we can find an explanatory one. Further studies were made from which it became clear that the relationship between the number of vehicles on a given route which use the petrol station was related to the added time to the journey. This added time is not the 'real' added time but rather the added time as perceived by the driver.

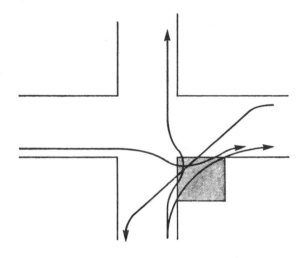

Figure 14

There are standard results in psychology which show the relationship between this real time and the perceived time and when real time was eliminated and substituted by perceived time and relationship was very close. One now had an explanatory model rather than the descriptive one which had been first obtained. (It is parenthetically interesting to reflect that such a model as this enables one to do more than was originally intended. For example, part of the understanding of the industry had been that petrol stations at a road junction took up most of the potential sales there and would pre-empt the development of any other stations at the same junction. However, as can be seen for the petrol station in the diagram above, it would not consume any of the three major sales routes for a station at any one of the other three corners. It now becomes feasible to buy sites at junctions where there is already a station, because it is not realized by competitors that the sales potential there is just as great and the sites in question will be going more cheaply.)

The explanatory model in particular does enable us to dispose of a main objection to results based solely on a descriptive model in this case. But it cannot be too strongly emphasized that we must always, wherever possible, seek the explanatory model.

4.

The fourth category is the situation where it is not possible to isolate the effects of individual variables and it is necessary to experiment. The typical areas where this occurs are the allocation of effort in research and development, and also problems in the general field of marketing. In both these cases we have areas which, although they must have an underlying structure, as far as our present state of knowledge is concerned are ill-structured. We shall be taking these problems in more detail in the chapter on marketing which follows but we present here the classic example which Ackoff adduces, namely his work on the relationship between advertising for beer and the sales of beer.

It is a fair assumption that with increase of advertising there would not be any decline in the sales of a product. Hence the first model which is derived or proposed in these situations is always of the type shown in Figure 15.

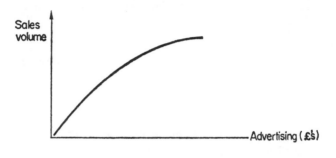

Figure 15

In the case in question the company had been advertising on television at a constant level for some period of time and sales had been fairly constant. Hence the graph in Figure 15 could only be put through one point.

Experiments were then performed to raise and lower the level of advertising by fifty per cent in different parts of the country. As a result the sales in those areas where advertising had been increased by fifty per cent showed a significant

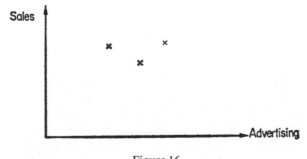

Figure 16

improvement and the sales in those areas where advertising had been decreased by fifty per cent also showed a significant improvement. Clearly the original hypothesis is no longer tenable. When such results occur we must be careful to study the data, for whenever common sense is apparently rejected the most likely reason is that our data are wrong or have been analysed incorrectly. Careful analysis however showed that there were no errors in the data and hence the hypothesis was now proposed that it is possible for people to be repelled by too much advertising. Hence the advertising response curve may be as shown in Figure 17.

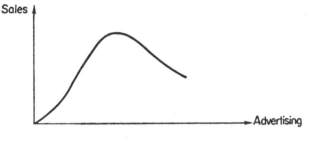

Figure 17

Clearly, however, even this is not consistent with the results which have been shown by the experiment but it would be consistent if the population could be taken as falling into two main classes, the confirmed beer-drinker and the light beer-drinker, each with a different response curve (see Figure 18).

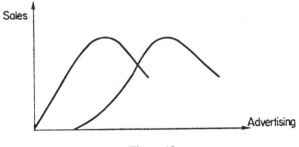

Figure 18

The sum of these curves would then give a relationship as shown in Figure 19.

A complete set of experiments in raising and lowering advertising rates in different areas, particularly when linked to the hypotheses as to the proportion of population that would lie upon either of the two basic response graphs, showed an accurate relationship which confirmed the hypothesis. Whenever we carry out such statistical experimentation it should always be against a

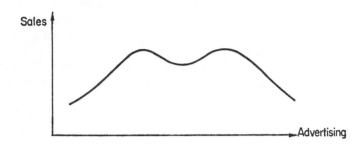

Figure 19

basic hypothesis. This is particularly necessary as we are in general overwhelmed by alternative variables which we might consider. Where the hypothesis is rejected, however, we must be careful to check whether common sense has gone wrong. It is in these cases that the power of the model-building approach lies.

5.

The fifth category which Ackoff and Sasieni propose is that in which sufficient descriptive data are not available and experimentation is precluded. In these circumstances our only approach can be via a thorough understanding and formulation of basic hypotheses and by formulating experiments which we can manipulate. In these situations the methods of simulation are of great power. Much gaming is in this field, and in many cases marketing too will fall into this category. Ackoff suggests that social problems are most likely to fall into this field. One of the best ways to check on the hypothesis in a model is to invite those experienced in the field to manipulate the simulation, and ask them whether it 'feels' and sounds right. One can formulate experiments to see whether the simulation is responding with the time lags and with the characteristics of the natural system (See Chapter 11).

Sometimes it is possible to use a simulation based on a combination of real life-real time data and hypothetical guesswork. An example of this was a study by the O.R. group at the National Coal Board which must have been one of the first applications of simulation (see Clapham & Dunn[11]).

The problem arose in estimating the time to clear a coal mine in an emergency and to estimate how this time might be reduced by reorganising the underground telephone system. It is through this system that all messages proceed as it is necessary to give precise instructions as to the route to be taken to pit bottom so as to avoid foul air. It was impossible to have dummy runs for evacuating the pit and *a fortiori* impossible to experiment with different layouts of the telephone. Data were collected on the routine day-to-day working of the system, particular emphasis being given to estimating the probability of a call being unanswered. In some locations this could be very high and if it occurred in an emergency a runner would have to be sent from another point. Trial imaginary evacuations, using first of all paper, pencil and tables of random numbers and, later on, a computer (which was hot stuff in 1954), were performed from which the rate of withdrawal from a particular pit could be estimated and the effect on this rate of changes in the layout of the phone system were predicted.

A further classification

We now present a possible alternative way of looking at the classification of structures of models. There seems to be a fundamental difference between those model situations in which there is some form of feedback by which the variables affect the condition of the system and those in which the selection of the variables, particularly the controllable variables, do not have any effect on the system. It should be emphasized, at this stage, that the nature of this feedback which we now consider is separate and distinct from that of any control system which is operated in terms of implementing the model solution. All control systems have to involve feedbacks, which take the results of predicted decisions and monitor them against the actual decision by means of subsequently changing the level of the controllable variables. In this form of dichotomy we take the 'natural' relationships between the variables and estimate the extent to which they operate in a feedback manner. It might be instructive to look at the Ackoff-Rivett classification of models at the beginning of this chapter and see the extent to which they fall into the feedback and non-feedback classifications as now suggested.

1. *Queuing problems*

In most queuing problems we assume that there is no feedback. For example, if queue arrivals are undeterred by the length of the queue then there will not be feedback arising through the arrival intervals. Similarly if those waiting in a queue are not subsequently deterred and leave because they have waited more than a certain amount of time, again there will not be this feedback in effect. Equally it is always assumed that the service time is independent of the length of queue. It is in fact a human feature that not only is service time likely to decrease as queuing length increases, but also because of the desire to spread out the work over a slack period, there may well be a tendency for service time to increase when the queue length is shortened. In all these situations the feedback will operate and hence the structure of the queuing problem, as suggested at the beginning of this chapter, has to be modified as shown in Figure 20.

The example of the barber shop on page 44 is an illustration of this possible feedback effect.

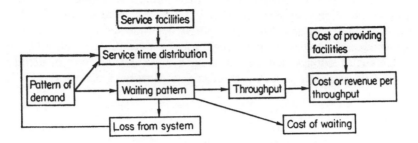

Figure 20. Modified queuing structure

2. *Inventory problems*

The case where feedback may occur in inventory problems is one which is ignored in most inventory control theory. It is to be expected that as the rate of demand for an item increases then the lead time for replenishment would also increase. The reason for this is that if our demand for the item is changing, then we will be making an increased demand on our supplier for replenishment. However, it is likely that all the others who are consuming the same item will also be increasing their demand. The effect of this on the supplier will be to increase the lead time. In these cases the usual cause-effect structure for an inventory problem previously presented has to be modified (see Figure 21).

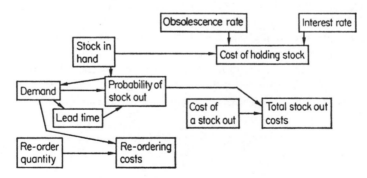

Figure 21. Modified inventory structure

3. *Allocation problems*

It is always the case in allocation problems that we assume a determinism in which the effect of a given allocation of resources is not going to manifest itself in any change in the reaction of the system to this allocation. Even in those allocation problems where there is a probabilistic basis we will still stipulate that the parameters of this probability distribution do not change over time, as a result of the actual allocation we are undertaking. It will be seen later that in many cases there is a form of feedback in an allocation problem, because of the change in the state of nature with which we are dealing. In most of the allocation problems, which are purely deterministic however, particularly those which are dealt with by mathematical programming methods, we will find that such feedback does not take place. We can therefore, particularly in deterministic areas, classify allocation as a non-feedback problem.

4. *Scheduling and routing*

It is a feature of all scheduling and routing problems that the reaction of the system to the particular policy we undertake, either in scheduling or in ordering a routing is independent of the actual decision taken by the decision-maker. These problems therefore will clearly be of a non-feedback type and the type of structure as suggested above will apply.

5. *Replacement and maintenance*

The system here is purely 'mechanical', that is, insentient. Hence feedback cannot apply, unless the quality of workmanship in maintenance is affected by the amount of demand for work.

6. *Search problems*

In this area we have to create a clear distinction between two types of problems. There are first of all search problems in which the environment in general and the thing being searched for in particular may react against the strategy of the searcher. If this is the case, then there is a feedback-type problem. On the other hand, in most cases where search theory is developed we assume a static environment and a static response of the target; that is, the actions of the two are uncoupled, and hence we will then have a non-feedback situation.

7. *Competitive problems*

It is sufficient at this stage to repeat the clear distinction between two types of competitive problem. There are those in which the reaction of the competitor and of the environment is so sluggish that we may regard the competitor as part of nature itself. These situations then will clearly be of the non-feedback type. There are other competitive problems however in which there is a fast reaction by the competitor (by fast we mean one that lies within the planning horizon over which we are estimating the consequences of our decisions). In these cases feedback is present.

As was stated at the beginning of this chapter, one of the reasons, perhaps the only reason, for having any form of classification of a model is to enable us to make reference to similar past situations which are likely to be relevant, and also to recognise those rare situations where a standard technique is capable of implementation. Perhaps because of this, the above classification, which is put forward rather tentatively, may be thought to have some merit within it. For example, in all those cases suggested above where natural feedback may apply it is probable that the methodology involved in the solution of the problem will entail some form of simulation. In those cases where such feedback is not present, it is more likely that the form of solution will involve either a direct appeal to standard mathematical and statistical methods or the mathematical methods as used in deterministic situations. Even, of course, where we have to appeal to a simulation approach, one of the objectives of such an appeal will be to reveal the sensitive parameters and to see whether the feedback itself is affecting the system in any marked way. If it is not, then recourse can be made to the standard mathematical techniques.

How is it done?

Assuming that we can diagnose a particular problem as being in one of the above categories (and remembering that the most interesting and important problems probably lie outside these categories), what are the questions we should ask at the start of a piece of research?

1. *Queuing*

How many service points?
What are the distributions of service time at each of them?
Are these distributions stationary over time? If not—what affects the non-stationarity? Does this imply feedback? (If so the 'normal' theory will not apply and we simulate.)
What is the form of the queue discipline?
What is the distribution of time btween successive arrivals?
Are there two objectives involved—server and served?
If so, can we resolve the conflict between the two?
If there is only one objective—is the mechanism of the resolution satisfactory?
List the controllable and uncontrollable variables,
how sensitive is the performance of the system to changes in the controllable variables and to our forecasts of the uncontrollable variables?

2. *Inventory*

Forecasts of demand? Can we refine these forecasts?
Forecasts of lead time? Is it correlated with demand? (If so there is feedback and normal theory does not apply.)
Check whether review system is cyclic or two bin.
What is probability of running out during level time?

How is this cost estimated—per item, per day or per item-day?

Remember this is a very fuzzy opportunity cost. Does a change in it have a significant effect on the over all cost?

What is stockholding cost? How is it calculated? Is it based on the cost of borrowing money, the profit of lending money (i.e. of investing cash in our own business) and which of these costs or profits is used, and why?

How is re-order cost calculated—is it marginal cost, average cost, or opportunity cost? And why?

What is the set of constraints, e.g. number of stockholding points?

Can they be eased?

3. *Allocation*

What are the resources, how are they measured and what limitations are there upon them?

What is the set of tasks to perform and what are the sets of objectives?

Can these objectives be brought into one common measure?

If so, how valid is the transfer function and how sensitive is our answer to it?

What are the constraints on objectives, tasks and resources?

If these involve continuous linear functions, independent of time, examine carefully the reality and sensitivity of continuity, lineararity and time independent.

4. *Scheduling and routing*

What is the optimum breakdown of the total task into elements?

How coarsely can we do this?

What is the relationship between these elements?

Can we measure the cost of different orderings of these elements?

What are the constraints on the resources involved and can we measure the return of relaxing these constraints?

What is the objective?

Is it measured in the same units as the elements and the constraints?

If not, can we solve the problem of relaxing the constraints?

5. *Replacement and maintenance*

What is the cost of failure? Is it a once-for-all cost or does it depend also on the duration of failure?

What is the cost of maintenance?

What is the probability of failure and is it affected by maintenance?

Is this probability stationary?

6. *Competition*

What are our objectives and how do they cohere or conflict with our competitors?

What are the units of measurement?

What is the time horizon?

Over what period of time will our decision have consequence?

Are these decisions reversible?

Is the response of the competitor likely to be fast or can we treat the problem as one of allocation?

If the former, what are the relative pay-offs to us and our competitor(s)?

What do we know of his (their) psychology and how likely is escalation of a prisoner's dilemma type?

What is the stability of the situation?

If the latter, what are the constant resources within which we are allocating?

What are the pay-offs of various allocations—are they linear or non-linear continuous or discrete, do the successive decisions interact?

5 Accounting Data

'Wine makes merry, but money answers all things'
Book of Ecclesiastes

EVERY MODEL builder appreciates that it is rare for the cost data which are available in an organization to be appropriate or relevant to his investigation. The reason is that data which are kept for purposes of day-to-day control are seldom based on the assumptions which are required when one is extrapolating into the future and considering the likely consequences of alternative courses of action. Nevertheless the use of money as a transfer function, by which resources and results can be compared, is extremely convenient and in every investigation the model builder will seek to express the final results in as few incommensurable variables as possible. Consequently the operational research scientist will have to work in close cooperation with the accountant and in doing so it is necessary to be frank about the way this relationship has expressed itself so far.

It would be an exaggeration to state that the scientist regards the accountant in terms of great affection. The accountant is generally looked on as 'a rather dull, grey figure who acts as an impediment to useful and dynamic development. He acts as the keeper of the conscience and is rarely seen as a lively man eager to see the future take place. The picture of the accountant as a worried figure walking backwards into the future while looking carefully at the past is an exaggeration but has a grain of truth within it. Nevertheless the greatest treasurer which a scientist can find is a lively, modern-minded accountant. This man will be worth the world and should be treated accordingly.

It might be instructive to survey some of the reasons why the accounting profession exists and has developed in its present way. Until the first industrial revolution most companies were owned and managed by the same man. The industrial revolution stemmed from the development of power generation equipment and machine tools and these increased the capital needed to start and to run a company. This meant that the single owner-manager tended to be replaced on the ownership side by a group of shareholders. This group of shareholders would demand assurance and reassurance that their money was being properly used. For this reason the accountant initially came into prominence as an honest book-keeper. As business becomes more complex mere book-keeping skills were no longer enough and the accountant began to develop a fairly sophisticated range of aids, generally of an arithmetical nature. Soon however it became more difficult to have precise standards of costing and valuation applied to widely different circumstances. Consequently we have seen the development of different concepts over the last twenty years, until at the present time it is true to say that it is meaningless to talk of cost, profit, revenue, profitability and so on as physically measurable without at the same time stating the underlying assumptions of the measurement.

As the incidence of tax on business increased, it became necessary for accountants to develop and offer skills as tax advisers. Whereas in the United States there is a controversy between the lawyers and the accountants as to who should be giving tax advice to companies, in this country the accountant has an almost completely clear field. The development of tax skills came, therefore, as another arm in the accounting profession and to a large extent, until recently, the training of the accountant has been devoted to the two fields, of auditing (that is to give assurance to the shareholders that the money and the assets are really there) and, on the other hand, of tax advice (so that the Inland Revenue can deal as professional with professional in this area).

So far as some of the large public accounting practices are concerned, the last twenty years have seen developments beyond this. The development of the data processing equipment, which has spearheaded the second industrial revolution, meant that accountants were concerned not only with costs and valuation but also with the systems by which these costs and valuations were derived. From a first beginning of interest in accounting systems generally, they led to the knowledge of automatic and electronic data processing systems with, of course, a need to understand clearly the accounting uses of computers. Consequently most of the large practices offer advice, not only on systems of accounting but also on computer installation and will often provide a programming and software service. Of course, data are used as a means not only of giving reassurance to shareholders but also as a way of enabling better decisions to be undertaken with the company. Consequently accounting firms have become interested in such developments as method study, systems analysis, profit appraisal and operational research. The development of additional consulting work by the accounting firms has been rapid and in some of the large accounting offices, the profits stemming from the management consulting business may compare with that from the more classical and routine audit and tax functions. We are seeing, therefore, in the accounting profession, a diversification of skills offered although, alas, the routine training of accountants through articles in order to pass the professional examinations of the relevant Institutes has not really kept up fully with the progress in other fields. Only recently have accountants, through their professional Institutes, recognised the needs for research into accounting principles and practices. Without such research the profession would become sterile and wither away.

As can be seen, therefore, the historical development of accounting, which still accounts for most of the routine functions of the accountant, has been in dealing with the ownership of organizations, that is what has been referred to as the act of reassurance, and also in dealing with tax. This has meant that historically most work has been in the fields of asset valuation including the valuation of capital goods and the valuation of stocks. There has also been concern with the way in which the future should be safeguarded with particular reference to carrying forward in any accounting period the debts which the company will have to meet and being careful about carrying forward any expected profits which the company may accrue from current work in hand. This basically conservative approach stems naturally from some of the occasions in which, during the last hundred years, investors have been fleeced of their savings by unscrupulous businessmen. However, the events of recent years are not such as to reassure the investor that the situation is completely under control. But it is a useful start for the management scientist, in understanding the approach of the accountant to the problems in which they are both interested, to review the basic principles on which the accountant will base his findings. There are six of these basic and overlapping principles which can be summarized as follows.

1. *Conservatism.* We have referred in passing to this belief. It expresses itself in practice by always taking pessimistic of any viewpoint where alternatives are available. A liability will be recognised as soon as possible and its 'cost' brought forward. An income will only be accepted when it is realized. For example, if an asset is being valued then the principle of conservatism would lead to it being valued as modestly as possible. If there is a possibility of a company having to pay expenses for an as yet unknown liability then the principle of conservatism would be to write in these anticipated expenses at as high a figure as is 'reasonable'. Conservatism also means that even though there may be an income which should stem from work in hand, this income should not be brought into any present accounting period but should only be brought into the books when it is actually realized.

2. *Realization.* The realization convention is part of the principle of conservatism. We have referred to the belief that one should not anticipate revenue. In addition, for example, if part of one's assets is equity shares then those equity shares should be valued, under the principle of realization, at either the price that was paid for them or at the current market price, whichever is the lower. Thus, for example, if one had industrial shares for which £1,000 had been paid and the value of these in the market at the present time is £5,000, then they would be valued under this principle at £1,000. On the other hand if £1,000 had been paid for shares which were now valued at only £500, then the principle of realization would be that they should be valued at the lower figure of £500, if there was thought to be a permanent diminution of value to this level. Conservatism may well lead to accepting a depressed value for such shares.

3. *Objectivity.* The principle of objectivity recognizes the audit function as being based on expressing value and admitting asset value only to those

things which can be seen and checked. Consequently, this has led to accountants using historical cost even though the whole world may recognize that inflation is a continuous process. The principle of objectivity applied to stock recognizes only the documents which state what was paid for the stock on hand and will not recognize market value unless it is below cost. Hence historical costing has often been the basis of accounting procedures.

4. *Consistency*. The doctrine of consistency states that the processes by which costs, revenue, profits and profitability are derived should be constant from year to year. If the accounting basis changes then full disclosure will be made by the auditor in his certificate providing the client company agrees. However, the basis on which costs, profits and profitability are accounted at any period of time have not always appeared in a balance sheet statement. Thus one has no knowledge of the processes by which the figures in the balance sheet have been obtained; all one is told is when a change has occurred. Consequently although it is possible to compare the successive years' performance of a company over a period of time, it is not possible in any meaningful way of compare the performance of different companies over the same period of time.

5. *Full disclosure*. The principle of full disclosure requires that in any set of accounts which the accountant prepares for those outside an organization, there should be a full disclosure and discussion of all the relevant information. As has been seen from the remarks on consistency, this does not always take place. Some companies give full information on the basis of the way in which valuation of all their assets, for example, have been derived. But the use of historical costs in any full disclosure statement is of such limited value as to render this principle as being almost continuously violated in every audit statement.

6. *Materiality*. This principle sets bounds to the full disclosure above. It states that the only items which need to be discussed or disclosed in any statement, are those which are material to the purpose of the statement.

It is in the light of these principles that we can now review the way in which the model builder is likely to meet them in the methods by which the accountant derives his costs and revenue statements.

It will be convenient to observe how accountants may treat costs and revenues in different ways by starting from the smaller decisions and building up to the total profits picture.

A. *Valuation of stocks*

Suppose we have raw material stocks which have been built up over a period of time by buying raw material at different prices from time to time. The production line is serviced by these stocks. Two problems arise. The first is the way in which these stocks can themselves be valued. There are a number of approaches to this. We can, for example, assume that the valuation of the total stock corresponds with the current market price for the raw material, although this is rare. Alternatively we can assume that the pool of raw material is being drawn from the order in which the raw material was purchased, and hence we can keep a runing valuation of stock in terms of the price that was paid for each unit. Finally we can value at the price that would be obtained if the stock were sold at today's prices. There are thus three bases on which the value of stock can be formed. They are the cost of buying the stock in question, the cost of replacing all the stock at today's current price and thirdly, the proceeds which would accrue if all the stock were sold. In practice the lowest of these three would probably be taken.

The valuation of stock representing work in hand, and in particular partly processed work, is rather more complex. One can take an average cost of the stock represented by the average purchase price of the raw material, with some form of added value stemming from the production cost which has been put into the raw material. One can value the raw material which has gone into the process stock on a first in, first out basis so that the raw material is valued at today's current price. Finally one can take as the value of the in-process stock a figure which fully represents the total overheads which have been allocated to the production in question together with the variable costs of production and the raw material costs. There are therefore three ways of costing out in-process stocks, each of which can be combined with the three broad bases mentioned earlier.

One link between stock value and raw material cost arises when withdrawals are made from raw material stocks to service a production line. A curious paradox arises. The principle of conservatism applied to valuation of stock may require the value to be based on the lowest price paid for the stock. Indeed if raw material prices are falling, present day price would be used; but such prices applied to the cost of raw material in costing out production costs would, because they use a minimum cost, violate the principle of conservatism and a higher figure might then be used in production costing from that used in stock valuation.

B. *Product costing*

We now have the difficult question of the way in which products should be costed out. If we take the crude division of the total costs of a plant as between the fixed costs and the variable costs, we find that the fixed costs include the total plant depreciation, rent, heating, lighting, cost of capital, perhaps an allocation of head office overheads, as well as supervisory and managerial labour. The variable costs will be related to specific production time on specific machines, together with the costs of the raw material. What goes into a variable cost is open to question. For example, one can ask the question whether machine labour is a fixed cost (which it is if there is no hire and fire policy) or whether it can be treated as a variable cost being directly related to the work carried out on the machine. It is then tempting to take the cost of a new item which is going to be made on a production line which has spare capacity, on a straight marginal basis. It is certainly true that in terms of the increased cost to the company of making this new item, this can be regarded solely in marginal terms. On the other hand, however, someone somewhere has to bear the cost of the overheads and if we cost out the production of different units in the way which is suggested then we will find that the cost per item produced would depend upon when the item in question was first scheduled for production. The first item made on the line will bear the full overhead costs while those which follow will only bear the marginal costs. This clearly is unreasonable. There might be force in the argument that one should take the cost of a production line on a total basis and merely cost out a total batch of work of different type against a total cost of the plant. If one does this, then the selling price is not necessarily going to be related to the production costs, since we are avoiding allocating a cost for producing any particular part of the total products mix. The selling price will be based on what the market will bear, but then it will be difficult to see whether marketing efforts should be switched from selling one line to another in terms of the real contribution which the different lines are making to production. It is also difficult in these cases to set a proper selling target for the sales force. If a sales force is judged by contribution to profit of what it has sold, then it is necessary to know for each item offered what the specific contribution is to profit. We shall then be forced into calculating unit-pricing by dividing out the total product mix cost into various lines which are worked through the production process.

One should therefore be very careful, when asking the cost of production for a particular unit, to make quite clear how the overheads have been allocated and how the total costs have been acheived. The problem is sometimes made more complex because raw material may be bought in batches of mixed qualities. This is sometimes done in order to buy quality material at a lower price by accepting, in a batch of mixed quality, some low quality raw material. How one should allocate the purchase price between these mixed batches of raw material and hence derive an estimate of total production costs on which selling price and profitability of sales may be based, is clearly a very complex problem to which there is no obvious single answer. What is necessary, however, is that in looking at production line problems the operational research worker should be quite clear how costs and revenues have been treated, and also in terms of any new decisions which may be undertaken, whether the costs and revenue stemming from these new decisions are in the opinion of the model builder adequately reflected so as to guide decisions correctly.

C. *Total plant costs*

In estimating the performance of a particular plant, which may sometimes be needed in order to evaluate further investment in a company, it is of course important not only to have a firm understanding of the allocation of costs and revenues, but also to see the way in which the performance of a plant over a given period of time is reflected by the anticipation of revenue. For example, over a number of years a particular factory may have a large amount of its production capacity allocated to long term work for which income will only be received upon completion, which may be outside the financial years in question. If this is so, the financial profitability of the particular works may be down-graded because the principle of conservatism will carry forward the value of the work in hand and semi-finished work far below its ultimate realizable figure.

Three other factors have to be considered of a more macro nature. The first of these is the effect of inflation. If the money base is changing then we are measuring quantities by a ruler which is constantly shrinking in size. Consequently there will be grave dangers in accepting historical costs over a period of time, as though the value of money has not changed. In any period of inflation (to which we seem permanently committed) we will mislead ourselves if we treat money as being constant in value. Consequently heavy capital expenditure may well have an additional investment for the future because of the inflationary element. The principle of conservatism, while wise in discouraging over-optimism, may force a company into failing to recognise valid investment opportunities.

Two other problems arise. The first is the question of depreciation, which is always a form of saving. Basically depreciation is doing one of two things. Either we are currently saving in order to have enough money on hand to replace an asset when it is worn out, or alternatively we are currently saving to pay off the loan against which we originally sought in order to buy the asset in question. Both of these calculations are carried out over what may be regarded as the real life of the asset. What the real life is may of course be subject to a very high degree of subjectivity. This is particularly the case in development expenditure when one is unsure whether a new product will have any market, and hence the real life of the machine which is specific to making that product may be extremely difficult to estimate. In these circumstances the accountant will normally adopt a conservative approach by depreciating the asset over a very short period of time. In many prior investment calculations this is sufficient to condemn the investment. One must be careful not to discount risk twice over. Sometimes one discounts risk by applying a high interest rate to money which has to be borrowed for a specific project and, in addition, one compounds the cost of the speculation by depreciating the equipment itself over a shorter period than is necessary.

It should be realized that in many cases the depreciation period may be merely the shortest possible life which the inland revenue will accept for tax purposes and may not be related to the real life of the equipment. The model builder, therefore, should be careful to enquire the basis on which depreciation has been evolved. In addition, of course, one should enquire whether the time period over which the asset was initially depreciated has now expired. It may be that the original selling cost, which was related to the early calculations of raw material cost, production cost, depreciation together with a mark-up for profit, will not be up-dated when the important depreciation element is removed.

The final question is the cost of capital, which is used in many calculations, particularly those involving some form of discounted cash flow. From reading the literature on discounted cash flow one is tempted to assume that within every company there is some infinite source from which money can be borrowed at a fixed rate of interest and an infinite sink which will generate a fixed rate of interest against money which is put into it. This is a myth. There are numbers of ways in which one can evaluate cost of capital.

First one can cost out capital according to the interest rate which the firm is currently being charged on money borrowed from the banks and other institutions. This means that the investment in question is going to be financed by money borrowed in the open market. A second approach is to take the current cost of capital as represented by the return to the shareholders. A third way of costing out capital will take it as at the rate at which other investments in the firm are currently generating returns. Costing capital on this average basis will relate investment to the current profitability and is a way of treating the firm as its own banker.

These three figures for cost of capital will, of course, all give different approaches to surveying investment. As stated in Chapter 6 the effect of a higher cost of capital on present worth calculations, is to render much more important the return in earlier years, and to discount the return in future years. It is therefore a way of dealing with risk, and in situations where an investment is thought to be speculative there is always a temptation for the accountant to put another one or two per cent on the cost of capital, as a way of reflecting the risk element.

How then does one draw all this together in looking at the total profitability of an organization? As can be seen there is scope for different ways of treating, by perfectly acceptable accounting principles, the whole of the total profit picture of a company. The elements over which there is quite a range of possible treatment cover the following three points.

1. *The valuation of the assets including plant, sites and raw materials.* All of these can be valued in different ways and some of the most spectacular take-overs in the past years have stemmed from perceptive financiers realizing that the book value of the assets of a company may well be written down far too conservatively and may be worth together more than the current share value of the company. It is perhaps in this particular area that the greatest range of approaches exists.

2. *Treatment of future revenue*. The way in which future forecasts of profit may be made are well known. On the other hand, we must always be careful of the way in which the current accounting figures can reflect income which has been generated by the work of past years, and hence is really not contributing to performance in the present year. There is also the manner in which anticipation of income can be made by writing up the value of partly finished work. It also means that the income figures for a company may vary widely over any period of time.

3. *Costing out part of the whole*. How are overheads allocated? What are truly marginal costs and revenues? What share of the costs should be born by each part? What is the marginal profitability of each further sale?

There is, however, one important point which must be emphasized. Where there are alternative methods the choice of which alternative to use is NOT an accounting problem. For example, the allocation of overheads in a production line between the different units which might be produced requires OR to evaluate alternative procedures. Selling price depends not on this cost allocation if there are different prices elasticities for the different units. Overall profits maximization, which is the objective, will not be achieved by basing price on some form of allocation of overheads.

Of critical importance is the matter of opportunity costing. This may not be important for audit and tax purposes but may be vital for managerial purposes. The change which is taking place in accounting is essentially a change of perspective, from the requirements of those outside the organization to the needs to those within.

We see, therefore, that whereas in the science concepts such as mass, velocity, volume are uniquely definable and measurable, a concept such as cost has no uniqueness. The cost of producing a book is related to the purpose for which the cost figure is going to be used but the mass of a book does not depend on purpose. It is this which the scientist finds confusing and discouraging. Never go to an accountant and ask for costs, revenues, profits without telling him why they are wanted and without asking the basis on which they are computed. This is necessary for all users of cost data including senior managers and directors who rarely ask for this basis.

There are always three costs—average, marginal, opportunity. The allocation of overheads and the distinction between fixed and variable costs may be murky. In decisions of value we may wish to reject the extreme conservatism of the auditor.

There are excellent discussions of these matters in Ackoff[12] and Churchman.[13]

6 Investment Choice

'I have neither lent on usury neither had men lent
to me on usury yet everyone doth curse me'
Jeremiah

IN THE previous chapters we have discussed the structure of models in general terms, the realities of pressures on the decision-maker, and the problems involved in creating the basic measure of the most usual transfer function money.

In this chapter we shall continue to explore the use of money. Clearly in the single stage deterministic case, if $x > y$ then we shall prefer £x to £y as a single receipt. Problems arise in deriving measures where either x or y is probabilistic or where cash is received over a period of time. Hence we are now concerned with measures expressing the attractiveness of single units (which we call money) when they are confounded with probability and/or time.

To generalise, we consider an initial investment a_0 (negative) at time $t = 0$, and cash returns (positive) or re-investments (negative) at equal intervals a_1, a_2, ..., a_n.

Simple investment models

At the beginning of this chapter we shall concentrate our attention on four of the most common methods of selecting the most attractive of a set of investments. In all these simplified cases we shall be taking the situation where we are investing money at one unique moment of time and this investment stimulates a return of cash. Hence we are dealing with a flow of cash which at any time may be either positive or negative. A positive flow of cash means cash is being returned to us from the investment, and a negative flow of cash means that at that moment money is flowing out from us to the investment. We have to formulate an estimate of what this cash flow is likely to be and this will generally be in the form shown in Figure 22.

The cash flow may be continuous, as above, as $f(t)$ say, or may be discrete a_1, a_2, a_3, ... We will always try to derive a single number which expresses the attractiveness of the flow of cash. There are four such single numbers which are commonly used. These are well known and will not be described here in any detail.

The average rate of return, which is very common, estimates the rate at which the investment is yielding money to us in terms of its initial cash input.

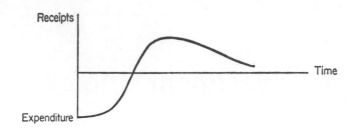

Figure 22. Cash flow as function of time

Hence the following two cash flows would have the same average rate of return.

A. Initial investment £100 in year zero.
Returns: £10 per year for 10 years, then £100 in year 11.

B. Initial investment £100 in year zero.
Returns: nothing for 10 years, then £200 in year 11.

Clearly the first of these two returns is more attractive than the second (neglecting the effects of inflation). The first flow yields money sooner which we can then use in some other investment opportunity. Hence, money is attractive not only in terms of its absolute value but also in terms of when we are likely to receive it.
    In algebraic terms:

$$\text{Average rate of return per period} = \frac{\sum\limits_{i=1}^{n} a_i}{n \, a_0}$$

Another equally simple method which is very widely used, is the pay-back period. A pay-back period is the time that elapses between making the investment and our receiving back the amount of the investment. It makes no reference, therefore, to the total amount of profit which is likely to be generated from the investment, nor to the rate at which there is going to be a return on the investment. Clearly in those cases where we get our money back more quickly there is a greater likelihood, through continuity of return, that we shall have a continuing, more prosperous investment than in those where money takes longer to be yielded. But there is also a simple reason why pay-back period is so widely used. This is that those administrators who are vulnerable because of investment decisions which they have authorized, may well be more attracted to those which are more likely to yield a quick profit. Once the profit is starting to flow in and the investment is paid for, then the pressure is off. Consequently the pay-back period is one which has a human reason for being used and, since all organizations consist of groups of humans acting and pressing on each other, it is not surprising that pay-back is popular.

In algebraic terms:

Pay back period is minimum k for which

$$\sum_{i=1}^{n} a_i > a_0$$

The two other methods make reference to the criticism made earlier about average rate of return, namely that they time at which money is returned is as important as the amount of money itself. The present worth criterion discounts future returns of cash. It does this by assuming a rate of interest which can be earned by the money which is yielded from an investment, once we have got it back. For example, if we say that money is worth 5 per cent a year to us, then £105 a year from now is going to be the same value to us as £100 is as of today. Hence all future cash returns in the notation above can be discounted at an interest rate to give a present value given by the formula

$$PV = \sum_{i} \frac{a_i}{(I + r)^i}$$

In continuous terms, if interest accrues and is compounded continually at rate r per unit of time, then suppose we have a sum a at time $t = 0$ which grows to an amount $g(t)$ at time t.

Now in time t, $t + \delta t$ g(t) will grow by $g(t)\,r\delta t$, that is $\delta g(t) = g(t)\,r\delta t$

i.e. $\dfrac{dg}{dt} = rg(t)$

giving $g(t) = be^{rt}$, where b is some constant.

But when $t = 0$, $g(t) = a$, hence $b = a$ and the growth of $g(t)$ under compound continuous interests is exponential — $g(t) = ae^{rt}$.

Hence the present value of a flow of cash $f(t)$ over the range $t = 0$ to

$$\int_0^T f(t)e^{-rt}\,dt$$

where a_i is the net return in the ith period and r is the rate of interest per period. The use of present worth calculations has become more widespread in recent years, but it is still subject to a number of criticisms which have been well documented by Adelson.[13] The problem of what value of r to use was discussed in Chapter 5.

Internal rate of return is at first sight very closely related to present work. In an internal rate of return estimate we state what the interest rate, r, would have to be, for the present worth of the future cash flow to be equal to the initial investment, I.

$$I = \sum_i \frac{a_i}{(I + r)^i}$$

The higher the internal rate of return, which is the root of the equation, the more attractive will be the investment. However, there are some difficulties about such a formula. It can be shown that in those cases where all the cash flows each year are positive, after the initial investment, there is only one real positive root of the equation. On the other hand if some of the years yield a negative cash flow, then there may be two or more such roots. In those cases the exact figure which one should use is not at all clear, although there are certain conventions as to which should be selected.[14] It might, however, be possible to take the cash flow up to, but not including, the first negative a_i. This flow will have a unique root for r above. The set of a_j which follow and which are negative can be looked on as a new investment, to be evaluated afresh.

Adelson[14] discusses critically internal rate of return and present worth.

Introduction of probability

It has so far been assumed that we know infallibly what is going to be the result of an investment decision over all the years up to our planning horizon. This clearly is not true. One should never use these models of investment selection in a deterministic way. How then should probability be introduced? The introduction of a variance figure on the return in any year is comparatively straightfoward, both in average rate of return and the pay-back period calculations. Such variances will in general increase as the investment returns recede further into the future. It is therefore more realistic to use some form of weighting coefficient on the investment, so that some notion of the actual credibility of the mean parameter will be introduced into the calculations in a way which is rather different from only introducing a larger variance. One such method would be to weight the return every year inversely as the sampling variance. This would have the effect of giving less credibility to returns in years far ahead in a way which is rather different from simply increasing the variance, and adding this in to the probability distribution of the return.

In present worth calculations methods have been devised to estimate the probability distribution of present worth, in terms of the probabilities to be associated with the estsimated returns of any year. Another way of looking at this same problem is by means of risk analysis. Some of the best accounts of this are given by Hertz.[15, 16, 17] In risk analysis we break down a total investment calculation into its component parts, rather in the same way that the total time to do a job is broken down into a network analysis calculation for a critical path appraisal and, as in a critical path, one estimates the mean and the variance of all the parameters which are used in the total investment calculation for a present worth. In addition, each of these parameters is assumed to have a probability distribution, which is also adduced a priori. Hence, for each of the parameters we require its expected value as in the present worth calculation, but also the mean and variance of the distribution of this expected value and the type of distribution itself. We then form a simulation run-through and select a variable from each of these distributions. From each of this set of particular values of the parameter we calculate the present worth corresponding to the set. In this way a number of successive selections from the separate parameter distributions each yields a present worth and so leads us to a distribution of the present worth.

This method is ingenious and focuses our attention on the effect of the variability of all the parameters which are used in the present worth calculation. It does however, yield a number of questions which the analyst must answer before placing a great deal of reliance on risk analysis. These questions can be listed as follows.

1. We assume that the deviations from the expected return yielded by the investment each year, are going to be independent of those in other years. Clearly however, if we have in a real investment one or two years in which the return is much less than we had anticipated, we would expect that we have been over-optimistic in general. We must therefore question the assumption which we have to make in most risk analyses (because of the complexity of not making it), that errors year by year are going to be mutually independent of each other.

2. The second question is the extent to which we are able to estimate the form of these prior probability distributions. The way in which it is recommended that we should estimate the distributions is to ask those concerned a series of questions from which we can deduce their form. For example, the man who is responsible for the building of a factory may be asked how long he thinks it is likely to take to be built. If he says he would expect it to be four years, we would then ask him to lay odds against it being more than five

years, more than four and a half years, more than three and a half years and so on. From this we would, in the approved manner, build a prior probability distribution.

Such procedures are fraught with danger. Some people are attracted by the idea of a gamble. To others it might appear, as it does to the present author, that the statement of probability of such a unique event is not clear in its meaning and difficult to estimate with any surety (see Chapter 8).

3. The third question stems from the second. This is the extent to which it is possible to forecast the probability of something which we are going to do ourselves. For example suppose I am asked the probability that while driving my car home from the university I will stop and buy flowers for my wife? I could probably give an estimate of this by studying my past behaviour. If I then had to take out a wager on the appropriate odds based on my probability estimate, then I am indeed in deep philosophical water. Finally, if the event were not buying flowers (which I have done frequently in the past) but a unique event in which I cannot have taken part before, then the philosophical water rises over my head.

It is unfair to ask those who are going to be concerned with an investment to estimate the probability of its success. The idea that we toss a coin into the air, and dispassionately stand by waiting to see if it comes down heads or tails is not the case. Once that coin is in the air every manager and executive is willing to come down heads or tails as the case may be. In the same way, once he has estimated a probability the manager continues to try to effect the probability.

4. There is another more general comment we can make about such investment studies. It is true that if we study a portfolio of stock, then what we paid for that stock is irrelevant in our deciding whether we sell any part of that portfolio and buy something else. In a dispassionate way what has already been spent on an investment project is also irrelevant in deciding whether that project should continue. However, in every real situation what has been spent is relevant to the decision-maker's problem of whether he should continue the investment. If he stops an investment, then he is going to be called to account for the money that has been spent and hence been wasted. There is, therefore, an inbuilt imperative in every investment to continue. In addition, a management achieves a degree of momentum associated with a particular investment project, and this momentum is important in influencing it to continue. The total organization is geared up to the expenditure and geared up to the expectancy of return. Consequently, all investment, once undertaken, will generate a continuing psychological pressure to allow that investment to continue. It need hardly be over-emphasized that many national and large scale company investments have been examples of this.

5. This leads to the final point. It is a feature of national life that the errors in return on investment tend almost always to be that we have initially been over-optimistic. Why should this be so? One is tempted to assume that those who carry out the initial calculations are incompetent. If so, then given the large losses which stem from such errors, it is surprising that these people retain their jobs. Perhaps this is not the reason. It may be that those who carry out the calculations want the investment to be agreed by the board and hence will always give the investment the benefit of every doubt. This is chicanery and it would be surprising if hard-headed directors and politicians did not discount in some way such calculations put to them. Perhaps, however, there is another reason. Some of the work of Hertz[15, 16] has shown that the distribution of internal rate of return, for example, obtained from a risk analysis calculation is such that the mean of the probability distribution is very much less than the estimate of internal rate of return based on the series of best estimates fo the individual parameters. In these cases the internal rate of return based solely on the best estimates will be a (highly) based estimator of the expected value of internal rate of return as derived from the probability distribution. It would be interesting for this area to be researched further, because it may be that the effect of errors in the estimates used in calculations, even for such simple parameters as internal rate of return and present worth, will give a very high bias to any estimate which is based solely on a series of best estimates for all the parameters involved.

All this illustrates why one should never accept any investment decision which is based solely on a deterministic approach to the variables involved. The problem of investment is fraught with probability and to treat it as a deterministic problem is to deceive oneself and, much more importantly, to decieve those whom the analyst is seeking to serve.

It may be objected that one cannot formulate any prior probability distribution of the parameters, as is done in a risk analysis. Even if this objection is sustained, and it is difficult not to sustain it, it is still the case that one should take various prior probability distributions and see what effect they have on the variablity of the ultimate decision parameter. An example of this is a sensitivity analysis in which the parameters in the internal rate of return or present worth calculations are varied in turn, and one observes the effect on the criteria of selection of changes in these parameters. This gives one, first of all, a feel for those elements of the calculations which are most sensitive in determining the criterion of choice and, secondly, gives one an idea of the credibility which can be placed on any such criterion. Two investments which yield estimated internal rates of return of, say, 15 per cent and 20 per cent may well be entirely within the sampling error of each other and the decision as to which should be undertaken can safely be made on other grounds.

The discussion has, perhaps inevitably, been critical. What should be done in practice? Firstly, we have seen enough to understand that one should never accept future income and expenditure figures in a fatalistic or deterministic manner. Probability statements should always be introduced either as in risk analysis or in the form of a sensitivity analysis. The effect of errors in the forecasts on the measure of choice should always be investigated. Secondly, an investment or a set of proposed investments should never be looked on as a closed set. The choice between them must be related to the set of past investments which are currently yielding returns. This is particularly important if forecasts of the 'stage of nature' are likely to affect pay-off. The introduction of 'hedging' investments which will reduce the overall variance of total return may be essential and such investments must then be selected not for themselves alone but for the effect of the new total set. Thirdly, because each method of selection of 'best' investment implies an objective function, we must always always ask why the investment is being made. The method of selection and criterion of choice should follow the statement of the goal and must not be allowed to subsume it.

7 Sequenced Decisions

'I do not wish to see the distant scene, one step enough for me'
Popular Hymn. *Lead Kindly Light*

Decision trees

The accepted treatment of sequences of decisions is by means of the technique of dynamic programming. This technique is well known and established, but its use gives rise to certain questions which the model builder must be able to answer. Perhaps we can illustrate these questions by means of a special use of dynamic programming in the form of a decision tree. We shall, however, question fundamentally the validity of the method. In a decision tree we take a sequence of decisions in which, after every decision is undertaken, there is a result and once that result is known there is the opportunity of taking a further decision. In diagrammatic form this appears as shown in Figure 23. Two forms of quantification is now introduced. At each node which corresponds to a point at which a decision has been taken, and for which we are now awaiting the result, a set of prior probabilities is allocated to each one of the possible consequences of that decision. Secondly at the end of each of the branches of the decision tree, a value is placed which represents the utility of arriving at that point. Sometimes, if a considerable time elapses between the first point of the tree and arrival at the end point on a branch, the value placed at the end of the branch will be a present worth of that point. These values take account of the costs involved in following the path to the particular and point and are taken as quantitative measures of the attractiveness of a particular end point.

The decision tree approach now enables one to decide what should be the first decision undertaken at point X. This is done by rolling back from the end point in the following manner. Take for example that particular branch of the tree above, which is shown in Figure 24.

Each of the probabilities for the state of nature, which may result from the decision taken at X, is multiplied by the value of the end point of the tree to give an expected value of being at that particular node. In this way expected values can be assigned to all of the last set of activity nodes. At each of the preceding nodes which now correspond to points of decision, the value of being at that point of decision will be the maximum of the expected values which stem from it, since if one were at that point of decision one would select the course of action which had the greatest expected value. Hence the above decision tree, in rolling back, gives a series of expected values at each of the decision points as shown in Figure 25.

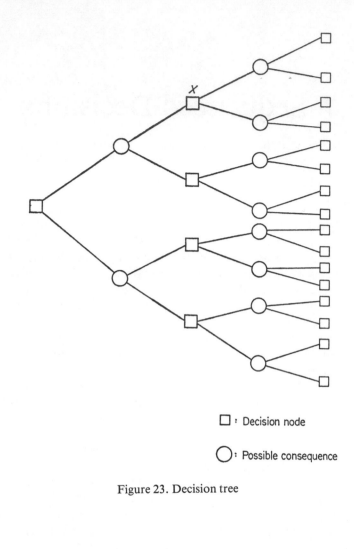

□ : Decision node

◯ : Possible consequence

Figure 23. Decision tree

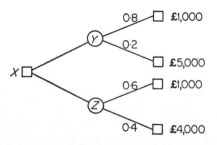

Figure 24. The decimal figures represent the prior estimate of probability. Expected value of Y is $0 \cdot 8 \ (1,000) + 0 \cdot 2 \ (5,000) = £1,800$. Expected value of Z is £2,200. Hence expected value of X is max $(1,800; 2,200) = £2,200$

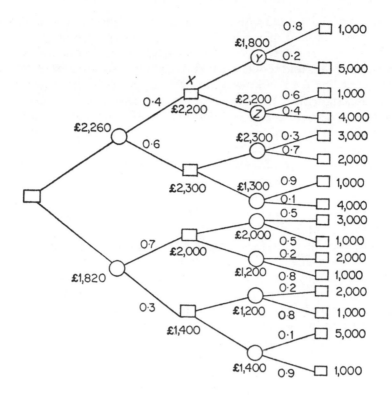

Figure 25

It is now possible, by using the total expected value of the decision branches at the origin, to select the best course of action. Having done so the decision-maker observes the result and, according to which of the possible results occurs, he will then select the next step from the options open to him. Hence he will advance through the tree on a series of alternate steps of decision, followed by observation, until he arrives at one of the terminal points.

Some criticisms

The questions which arise in this are appropriate to any discussion of dynamic programming as a method. First is the question of how one should select the actual decision points and how one should select the set of alternative consequences of each decision. As can be seen, the combinatorial problem involved, in having a wide range of decisions and a wide range of possible consequences, will be overwhelming. Consequently one does restrict choice severely and at each decision point one only allows a limited number of possible decisions followed by a limited number of possible consequences. One must question the robustness of the method with regard to the particular number of alternatives, both of decision and of result, that are allowed. A second question, is the effect of the particular timing of the sequences which one has allowed. In general, decisions and results are taking place in a continuum of time and we have adopted, in the decision tree, an arbitrary breakdown of time into points of decision and points at which consequences are observed and assessed. This may be of a decisive nature and before a decision tree approach is used one should enquire into the sensitivity of using the particular set of time-break points. Normally, of course, because of the combinatorial problem, one limits the total number of branches which can be allowed in the tree. Hence there is a correlation between the number of time-break points through the tree and the number of alternative courses of action and consequences which we allow ourselves. If we have fewer branch points we can allow more possible results at each branch point.

A third question is the way in which we derive a value to be placed at the end of each of the branches. These will depend on accounting conventions. They will certainly imply a large element of subjectivity in the way in which costs and revenues are estimated in a forward projection through the tree, and in addition we have to be quite sure why it is that we are using particular values. It may be that in some cases it is better to use a utility function approach. However, as can be seen from the discussion later in this chapter, there are certain concerns involved in using any particular form of value measurement.

Clearly at the heart of the decision lies the problem of estimating prior probabilities. Estimating probabilities is a skilled occupation and is not one to be undertaken light-heartedly. It is easy to persuade oneself that one has a valid estimate of probability but it is not often that the discipline of checking one's estimates of probabilities in the light of experience is allowed. In cases, for example, where in order to analyse a decision one has an estimate of the probability of an event occurring at say 20 per cent, it should be essential that the decision-maker should analyse historically all those decisions which he had estimated had a probability of 20 per cent to see whether, approximately, one in five of them occurred. There is sometimes a reluctance of the Bayesian statistician to submit himself to the discipline of posterior probability. As an illustration of the difficulty of estimating probabilities *a priori*, we can take the following well-known problem.

One is given a stick of unit length and asked to break it at random at any two points in such a way that each point in the whole length of the stick is equally likely to be either the first or the second break point. Having done this, one now has three pieces of stick and the problem is to estimate the probability of these three pieces forming a triangle. This is a well defined problem. Conceptually there is nothing difficult about it and indeed it is far simpler as a question than any of the questions that are asked of a decision-maker by the analyst, in estimating forward probabilities through a decision tree. We invite the reader to estimate this probability. Having done so he can refer to the end of this chapter to see how well he has done (but please do not look at the end of the chapter until you have made a subjective estimate of this probability).

For those who do not already know it, there is another illustration of the difficulty of estimating prior probabilities. In a room there are twenty-five people; what is the chance that two of them share the same birth-date (irrespective of the year of birth)? Here again is a well defined, well understood problem and the reader is invited to estimate this probability (which he will find at the end of this chapter).

These two examples should be sufficient to sound a note of warning when one is asked to estimate probabilities of events occurring. Naturally one does not wish to take a stance in which one refuses to estimate probabilities. Nevertheless it is, as has been indicated in the section on risk analysis, a most difficult task to perform, which has the disadvantage of seeming comparatively very simple.

There remains another, and possibly more subtle, question which has to be faced when a decision tree approach is used. In order for the dynamic programming approach to apply, or for the roll-back method to be applicable, it is necessary to be able to state beforehand what the decision-maker will do when faced with a set of alternatives at any stage of his progress through the tree. This is always assumed to be the selection of a course of action which maximizes the expected value of what may occur. However, there may well be circumstances in which a decision-maker is willing to take a risk and to select a course of action which does not have the maximum expected value. For example, suppose a decision-maker in moving through a tree has taken a particular series of decisions. The consequences of each of these has been unfortunate and he is now in a vulnerable situation. He may see a course of action which, although it has a remote chance of leading to a large gain, he would nevertheless select, rather than select another course of action with a greater expected value. This could be shown, for example, as in Figure 26.

In such a circumstance as this, it may be that the decision-maker would not be guided by expected value considerations. Such expected value considerations are more likely to apply when one is at the beginning of a whole series of random events, because over a series the choice by maximum expected value is more rational. However, if one has only one final opportunity of redeeming a bad position, the utility of the end points may now have changed. This then is the other comment that we should apply to a decision tree approach, namely that it makes the assumption that the values of the end point are going to be constant as we go through the tree, or alternatively any set of utilities given to those end points are going to remain unchanged. As can be seen this is not necessarily the case, and there may well be difficulty caused by imposing a structure of decision-making on a decision-maker to which he is going to feel obliged to adhere throughout a period of perhaps two or three years. To this extent one may well be rather uneasy about the prospect of using decision trees in any meaningful fashion.

A less misleading way of using a decision tree might be as follows. Firstly,

D

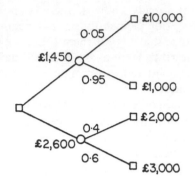

Figure 26

one should explore the implications of different trees with a cover of differing ranges of choice or consequence at each node and with differing numbers of stages to the horizon. (We note that if there are n exits from each node and there are m separate stages to the horizon, m being even, then for a given number of terminal states, $m \log n = $ constant. That is, it is in general easier to introduce complexity by reducing m and covering a greater range of n). Secondly, one should decide on the first decision in the light of what a number of such trees suggest and then review the whole future tree logic when the consequences of the first decision become clear. This will involve not only an examination of the m and n above, but also whether the horizon should be moved. For we note in practice that we very rarely reach the horizon — it becomes an objective rather than a time-oriented goal.

Answer to probability questions:

1. The probability of forming a triangle is 0.25.

2. The probability of a pair is (approximately) 0.5.

8 Utility Theory

'Singing songs of expectation'
Hymn: *Through the night of doubt and sorrow*

IN ALL decisions we expect three different concepts (at least) to be present:

(a) A unit of measurement.
(b) Probability.
(c) Time.

In some cases, in most mathematical programming, for example, we have (a) only, being fortunate to be deterministic and with no time effect. Time can be dealt with in many ways either seriatim as in decision trees or dynamic programming or by discounting a flow, as in present values. The combination of unit and probability is important not only because it enables us to study behaviour in the face of risk but also because the way of doing this (surprisingly) gives a method of dealing with more than one incommensurable unit.

Let us first consider behaviour in the face of risk and use as notation:

α, β, γ, are all positive numbers $0 < \alpha < 1$ etc.

x, y, z are all states of the universe (most often these will be sums of money).

$x \supset y$ means I prefer x to y.

$x \sim y$ means I am indifferent between x and y.

$\{\alpha, x; \beta, y\}$ is a gamble with probability α of winning x and probability β of winning y (if x and y are units such as money. x negative means I *pay x*).

Consider two simple gambles:

$$\{0.5, £100; 0.5, £0\} \text{ and } \{0.5, £50; 15, £40\}$$

The statistical expectations of these two are, respectively, £50 and £45, but it is not necessary for me to prefer the former. (Note there is nothing stupid or immoral in preferring one to the other, this theory is descriptive, not prescriptive.) If I do prefer the former, consider:

$$\{0.5, £1m; 0.5, £0\} \text{ and } \{0.5, £500,000; 15, £400,000\}$$

The expectation of the former is greater than the latter, but will I still necessarily choose it?

The point is that it is possible that statistical expectation of two gambles

$$A = \{\alpha, W; 1 - \alpha, x\} \text{ and } B = \{\beta, y; 1 - \beta, z\}, \text{ i.e.}$$
$$\alpha w + (1 - \alpha) x \text{ and } \beta y + (1 - \beta) z \text{ may be such that } A \text{ is preferred to } B$$
$$\text{and } \alpha w + (1 - \alpha) x < \beta y + (1 - \beta) z.$$

In this case can we find a transformation ϕ such that

A is preferred to B if and only if $\quad \phi(w) + (1 - \alpha)\phi(x) > \beta\phi(y) + (1 - \beta)\phi(z)$

This is the first problem to which we address ourselves. Its solution can give a lead to taking decisions between incommensurables. But first a detour is necessary.

We shall deal with the problem firstly by considering a series of lotteries with which we are going to be presented. In each of these we shall be offered a choice of joining in a lottery in which we are told there are two sorts of tickets, those that win and give us a fixed sum of money and those which lose and give us another (smaller) fixed sum of money. Sometimes this second sum is negative, i.e. we have to pay up rather than receive. We shall in every case be told the probability of our drawing a winning ticket and hence we can conceptually regard the lotteries as being situations in which we are offered the opportunity of putting our hand in a bag which contains a given number of winning tickets and a given number of losing tickets.

Consider a gamble in which we have the two possibilities: (i) of winning £100 with probability α; (ii) of losing £50 with probability $1 - \alpha$. For convenience this gamble will be denoted by $(\alpha, 100; 1 - \alpha, -50)$. Clearly if we were offered £100 for certain we would prefer this to the gamble. On the other hand we would prefer the gamble to the alternative of paying £50 for certain.

If $A \supset B$ denotes that A is preferred to B, then $100 \supset (\alpha, 100; 1 - \alpha, -50)$, and $(\alpha, 100; 1 - \alpha, -50) \supset -50$. Hence there should be some sum of money, say £x such that $-50 < x < 100$, at which we would be indifferent between being offered this sum for sure (if x is positive) or being forced to pay (if x is negative) and taking part in the gamble. This can be written

$$x \sim (\alpha, 100; 1 - \alpha, -50)$$

In this terminology x is called a CME (certain monetary equivalent). Thus, given any specified value of α, it is possible for each of us to state our own CME, x. There will then be for each one of us a functional relationship as shown in Figure 27.

The shape of the curve, $x = f(\alpha)$, will be an indication of the character and personal situation of its provider. A curve, above the line of expectation, indicates, an aversion to risk. The line $x = 150\alpha - 50$ is the expected value for any gamble with prizes of 100 and -50 and proportion of α of winning tickets. The abscissal distance of the difference between $(150\alpha - 50)$ and $f(\alpha)$ is a

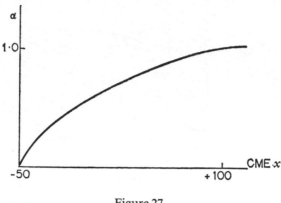

Figure 27

measure of the risk aversion as a function of α. As can be seen the more trivial the sum involved in the prizes the nearer should be the $f(\alpha)$ curve to the expected value line. Additionally, should the gambler know that he will have the opportunity of taking part in a sequence of such identical gambles (with differing α's) then his $f(\alpha)$ curve will approach the straight line, assuming he has reserves sufficient to meet any probable loss.

On the other hand, to many people gambling itself is attractive. No one would back a horse, play a casino or (especially) bet on football pools, whose indifference curve was concave upwards. Hence the horizontal displacement as in Figure 28 can also be a measure of risk attraction.

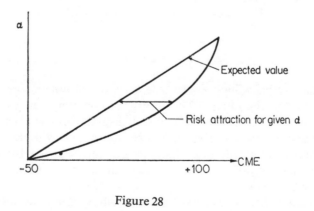

Figure 28

There can well be cases where a gambler may be risk averse at some probability levels and risk attractive at others. For example, the glory of pulling off a long shot may give such a curve as is shown in Figure 29.

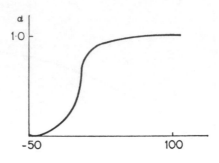

Figure 29

Of particular interest is the case of trading between two people with different indifference curves. For example a man who requires insurance against catastrophe will have a curve such as the one shown in Figure 30.

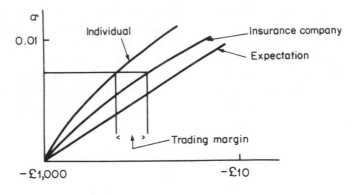

Figure 30

This expresses his willingness to lose a fixed amount (his premium) rather than take part in the lottery. The insurance company can work nearer the expected value curve and the horizontal displacement is then the expected profit to the company. Two such curves for two people with the corresponding horizontal differential will mean that bargains can be struck between them. In general, any pair of different indifference curves means that for the same α, bargains can be struck.

By using the indifference curve approach above it is also possible to show how any number of lotteries can be combined. Consider for example, a lottery in which we are offered a 20 per cent chance of winning £30, a 30 per cent chance of winning £10 and a 50 per cent chance of losing £25. This can be written schematically as in Figure 31.

From the indifference curve of the basic £100, — £50 lottery, we can now

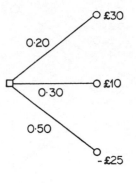

Figure 31

substitute for each of these tickets in the new lottery (i.e. for the £30, £10 and the —£25) the corresponding value of α read from the indifference curve. Hence, for example, if in the indifference curve we are indifferent between a fixed sum of £30 and the basic lottery with $\alpha = 0.8$, then we can in similar fashion for the £10 ($\alpha = 0.6$) and —£25 ($\alpha = 0.25$) prizes expand this new lottery as illustrated in Figure 32.

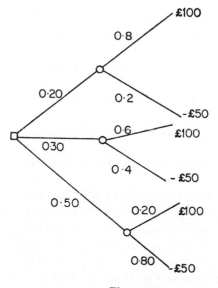

Figure 32

We can now contract this new lottery with its three kinds of tickets, into the diagram shown in Figure 33.

Hence, we have now transformed the original lottery into one in which there

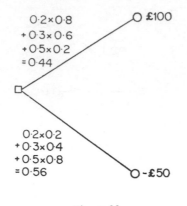

Figure 33

is a probability of 0·44 of winning £100 and a probability of 0·56 of losing £50. As can be seen in this way, any lottery with prizes lying within the range —50, 100, can be transformed into an equivalent basic lottery with these two extreme points as the two prizes. We can write this another way. Consider any basic reference lottery in which there are two prizes W and L, where $W>L$ and let the CME indifference curve for a lottery $(\alpha, W; 1 - \alpha, L)$ be $\alpha = \phi(w)$. Consider any other lottery with prizes x, y, where $L < y < w < x < W$.

Let the CME indifference curve for $(\alpha, x; 1 - \alpha, y)$ be $\alpha = \phi(w)$. Then

$$w \sim (A, W; 1 - A, L)$$

where $A = \phi(w)\{\phi(x) - \phi(y)\} + \phi(y)$.

But

$$w \sim (\phi(w), W; 1 - \phi(w), L).$$

Hence

$$\phi(w) = \phi(w)\{\phi(x) - \phi(y)\} + \phi(y).$$

This important result means that the CME indifference curve for any other lottery within the range (W, L) is that part of $\phi(w)$ lying between $(X; Y)$, where the vertical scale is magnified to $(0, 1)$. It also means, and this is extremely important, that we now have an additive law for these indifferences, for if $w \sim (\beta, x; 1-\beta, y)$ then $w \sim \beta Q(x) + (1-\beta)Q(y)$. This is fundamental to the utility theory approach to which we shall shortly turn.

A paradox

There is a danger that one may regard such an attractive build up of the basic logic of choices when faced with gambles as being one in which there will be consistency of choice. There is, however, an interesting paradox due to Allais. Consider two alternative choices: either £1m for certain (choice *a*) *or* the lottery (*b*) (see Figure 34). Which would the reader prefer—*a* or *b*? Consider now another pair of choices: either the lottery shown in Figure 35 (choice *c*) *or* the lottery shown in Figure 36 (choice *d*). Which would the reader prefer, *c* or *d*?

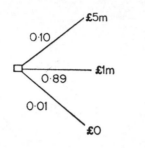

Figure 34

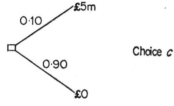

Figure 35

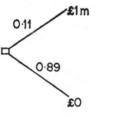

Figure 36

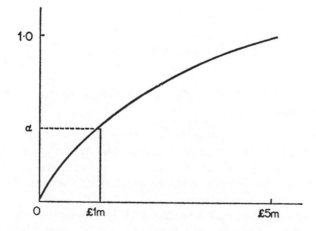

Figure 37

Let us analyse the choices and take as a basic reference lottery

$$L = £0, \quad W = £5m$$

Also let us assign the value α, such that £1m $(\alpha, £5m; 1 - \alpha, 0)$. Then the choice b is as shown in Figure 38.

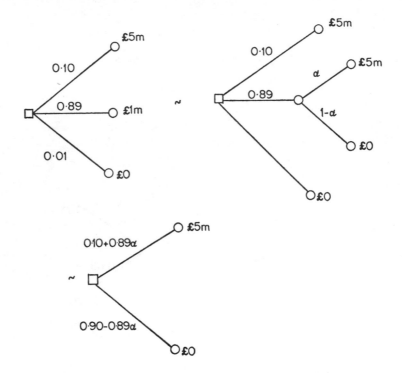

Figure 38

Hence if $a \supset b$, then $\alpha > .10 + .89\alpha$ i.e. $\alpha > \frac{10}{11}$ and vice versa. Similarly if $c \supset d$, then $\alpha < \frac{10}{11}$ and vice versa.

It is generally the case that most people when faced with these two sets of choices either select a and c or select b and d. The overwhelming number, in fact, prefer a to b and c to d. As can be seen from the above analysis, this is quite inconsistent, the value of α being contradicted if these choices are taken in this way.

What can one say about such a situation? It is tempting simply to say that the choice has been irrational and that one should mend one's ways. An alternative thought, however, is that although choice is irrational, maybe we have an inbuilt irrationality within us. Who is to say that we are in some sense morally wrong or even technically inefficient if we take these two choices of a and c? The theory as applied to these situations of choice should surely be such as to deal with our inbuilt preferences? If we have inbuilt preferences which in this way are shown to be illogical, is it necessarily the case that we should somehow improve and become less illogical?

The Von Neumann and Morganstern axioms

We now make a break in the continuity of this chapter and consider certain postulates and conclusions which stem from them in the field of utility theory. The object of utility theory is to study preferences and values and to show the assumptions that are necessary to enable such preferences and values to be represented in numerically useful ways. Consequently utility theory is concerned with trying to erect a calculus which can deal with personal preferences and with judgements of preferability, worth, value and goodness.

Over the years there have been a number of approaches to such a theory. We shall take the approach of Von Neumann and Morganstern.[18] They derived a basic set of axioms from which can be deduced the existence of mathematical functions which will have useful properties in comparing alternative states of the world in terms of their worth, value and goodness and general attractiveness to us.

It will be necessary first of all to state a notation which we shall use and then we shall present the basic axioms.

Notation:

x, y, z are states of the universe

$x \gtrsim y$ y is not preferred to x

$x \supset y$ x is preferred to y

$x \sim y$ We are indifferent between x and y or x and y are equally desirable.

α, β are real numbers; $0 < \alpha < 1, 0 < \beta < 1$.

The nine basic axioms which are necessary are:

1. For any x and y; either $x \supset y$ or $y \supset x$ or $x \sim y$

2. If $x \supset z$ and $z \supset y$; then $x \supset y$ (the transitivity axiom)

3. If $x \supset y$ then $x \supset (\alpha, x; 1 - \alpha, y)$ for any α

4. If $x \subset y$ then $x \subset (\alpha, x; 1 - \alpha, y)$ for any α

5. If $x \supset z \supset y$ then $\exists \, \alpha$, such that $(\alpha, x; 1 - \alpha, y) \supset z$

6. If $x \subset z \subset y$ then $\exists \, \alpha$ such that $(\alpha, x; 1 - \alpha, y) \subset z$

7. $(\alpha, x; 1 - \alpha, y) \sim (1 - \alpha, y; \alpha x)$

8. $(\alpha, (\beta, x; 1 - \beta, y); 1 - \alpha, y) \sim (\alpha\beta, x; 1 - \alpha\beta, y)$

9. If $x \sim y$ then $(\alpha, x; 1 - \alpha, z) \sim (\alpha, y; 1 - \alpha, z)$ for any α, z.

Von Neumann and Morganstern have shown that these axioms are sufficient to guarantee the existence of a real valued function ϕ such that

$$x \supset y \text{ if and only if } \phi(x) > \phi(y) \tag{1}$$

$$\phi(\alpha, x; 1 - \alpha, y) = \alpha\phi(X) + (1 - \alpha)\phi(y) \tag{2}$$

These two properties are essential for use as 'utilities' and are called the utility function properties.

If ϕ and ψ are two functions that satisfy (1) and (2), then it can be shown that $\psi(x) = a \, \phi(x) + b, (a > 0)$ i.e. a utility function is unique up to a positive linear transformation.

The reader can confirm for himself that these axioms are sufficient to validate the argument on pp. 88 to 92.

Discussion of the axioms

It is useful to discuss the implications of the nine axioms, especially in so far as they affect the validity of the utility theory approach as applied to model building. In model building we are concerned, amongst other things, with being able to select between alternative courses of action and we are also concerned with the problem of deciding between degrees of attainment of different competing objectives. It is useful to review the axioms one by one.

1. This axiom states that any two elements of the set of choices open to us are directly comparable. The consequence of this is that we must always be able to look at two alternatives and rank them in our minds by stating either that one is preferable to the other or alternatively that we are indifferent between them. It is important to be quite clear what is meant by this indifference. It does not mean that we are unable to choose between them. It means that we are able to observe their characteristics, to assess their characteristics and to conclude that either one set of characteristics is 'better' than the other or alternatively that they are equivalent to us. One

problem is caused by the fact that in some situations it may not be that we are indifferent between two alternatives but that we find it genuinely impossible to compare them. If, for example, we are concerned with statements of beauty, then I personally would find it impossible to distinguish between the beauty of a piece of music and, say, the beauty of a piece of literature.

2. The transitivity axiom seems, of all those stated, to be the most obviously reasonable and acceptable. Yet, there may be cases in which transitivity does not apply even to a situation in which there is logic and structure. Consider, for example, a committee consisting of three men, White, Brown and Black, each of whom is going to consider three investment opportunities while being each motivated in different ways. Each of the investment opportunities can be ranked according to three characteristics, say A, B and C. So far as White is concerned, he is only motivated by characteristic A and is indifferent between the other two characteristics. Brown is only motivated by characteristic B and is indifferent to the other two characteristics. Finally, Black is motivated solely by the third characteristic, C, and is indifferent between the other two characteristics. When the three investment opportunities are analysed according to the three characteristics, then Table 7 shows the ranking of the three investments against these three characteristics.

Table 7

Investment	Characteristic		
	A	B	C
X	Best	Worst	Medium
Y	Medium	Best	Worst
Z	Worst	Medium	Best

Remembering that White will vote only on characteristic A, Brown on B only, Black on C only, then if X is compared with Y it will receive the votes of A and C while B will vote for Y; i.e. $X \supset Y$.

Similarly if Y is compared with Z, it wins by two votes to one, i.e. $Y \supset Z$; but if Z is compared with X, it too wins by two votes to one, i.e. $X \supset Y \supset Z \supset X$. It must be emphasized that in reaching this paradoxical result each of the three committee men has voted consistently and logically. The fallacy, of course, is that given the symmetry of Table 7 there can be no choice which emerges as the best or the most acceptable. If any form of points scoring is used, for best, medium or worst, then obviously the points scored by each investment alternative will be the same. The voting, which is merely a form of ranking, ignores the fact that the single vote cast in each case corresponds to the greatest preference, that is 'best' compared with 'worst' while the other two votes compare with more modest preference. However, all the rules of choice have been followed and, as stated before, all one requires in utility theory is to be able to rank in a preference order. This is what White, Brown and Black have done and we have seen that this can lead to a paradoxical result.

The question of transitivity is particularly difficult. In logic it appears as an imperitive, behaviourally it can be a stumbling block. Stephen Clarke of Lancaster University has produced the following example* which is of interest.

Two dice are tossed. The higher number wins. A rational person might choose the dice with the higher probability of winning:

Dice A—Six sides are 0,0,4,4,6,6.
Dice B—Six sides are 1,1,1,5,5,5.
Dice C—Six sides are all 3.

Then the probability that A beats B is ½
B beats C is ½
C beats A is ⅓.
Then if offered pairs of dice a rational view would be

$$A \sim B, B \sim C, \quad A \supset C.$$

3. & 4. These two axioms together state that the act of gambling itself is not attractive. This, while being quite acceptable in the normal run of business decisions, is not necessarily an axiom which motivates individual conduct. A considerable gaming and betting industry exists because a large proportion of the population in a significant part of their activities do not accept these two axioms. Consequently since it is by no means sure that the managements of organizations have excluded all people who find gambling attractive in their spare time, we must be careful not to assume that these two axioms automatically apply. It is not necessarily the case that the executive leaves outside the office building his motivations and human passions that that between the hours of 9.00 a.m. and 5.30 p.m. he is motivated solely by reason.

5. & 6. These state that if X is preferred to Z and Z is preferred to Y then there is some gamble involving X and Y that is preferable to us receiving the Z for sure. This also assumes that the act of gambling does not affect our decision-making. For someone who is risk attractive there may be values of Z which are such that all gambles involving X and Y are preferred to it. On the other hand for someone who is very risk averse there may be a value of Z which is such that no gamble involving X and Y would be preferred to

*Private communication to the author.

receiving Z for sure. This axiom, like axioms 3 and 4, makes some important requirements on the consistency and the rationality of human behaviour.

7. This axiom states that the arrangement of the order of alternatives in a gamble is irrelevant to us. This has certain important behavioural assumptions. Thos carrying out card tricks, for example, know that the order in which one is asked to do certain things may affect behaviour. There may be situations where the order in which alternatives are presented to management affects their choice. Some research, for example, has already shown that the way in which people sit around a committee table affects the sorts of decisions which that committee might take and it may well be that the order in which a committee receives alternative propositions will affect the choice which they make. Consequently this particular axiom makes certain assumptions as to the cold-bloodedness of those who are observing the set of alternatives presented to them.

8. This axiom states that compound gambles can be decomposed by rules of the probability calculus. This strikes at the heart of the assumptions made in Bayesian statistics. The arguments used above, for example, to show the way in which compound gambles can be broken down and reduced to a single basic gamble, assume in some way that we can reduce compound situations in which probabilities exist only in our mind into physical lotteries in which we imagine tickets being placed in a box. It is a comment on the problems of deriving a calculus of credibility which is what the Bayesian statisticians are seeking to do, that in so doing they are inevitably pushed towards producing concepts which look remarkably like posterior probabilities. Although this is beyond the scope of the present discussion, it is undoubtedly the case that there is an urgent and growing need for statisticians (or perhaps, even better, non-statisticians) to derive a calculus of prior credibility which does not finish up looking remarkably like posterior probability statements.

9. This axiom states that if we are indifferent between X and Y, then if X appears in any gamble we can substitute Y for it without affecting our view of the desirability of the gamble. This makes the assumption, therefore, that if we are indifferent between X and Y we are going to be indifferent between them no matter what the surroundings. This is a considerably stronger statement regarding X and Y than those which are made in axiom 1 above. It may well be that the attractiveness of a particular alternative when placed before us is going to be markedly affected in our minds by the other alternatives which are open.

As can be seen from the above discussion (for a more extensive discussion see Churchman[12]), the assumptions necessary to derive a utility function are far more demanding than it at first appears. The question arises, as has been posed before, of the extent to which, if there is a lack of logic in the decision-maker when he is invited to subscribe to such an approach, we should regard the decision-maker as being illogical and therefore inefficient, or should we feel that the theory which we have produced is inadequate to deal with real situations? For in these most of the people involved are illogical, inconsistent and sometimes quite unreasonable. We shall return to this in a later chapter when we discuss some fo the problems and shortcomings of the operational research approach.

Utilities and gambles

Let us now return to the indifference curves for lotteries as discussed earlier. Suppose the x, y represent either scalar quantities such as money, or simply objects with a personal subjective worth. We require that we can rank all the x, y etc. in an order of preference. We can now derive a function that will have the characteristics (1) and (2) above (p. 81).

As can be seen the nine axioms are sufficient to enable us to state a CME indifference curve; moreover this indifference curve will have property (2) above, as seen previously. We now observe the importance of the additive nature of CME indifference curves in a lottery, for they form a utility function.

Alternatively it can also be seen that if $u(x)$ is a utility function of x such that if $x_1 > x_2 > x_3$ then let

$$u(x_1)[= 1] > u(x_2) > u(x_3)[= 0].$$

Now let x_2 be such that

$$x_2 \sim (\alpha, x_1; 1 - \alpha, x_3)$$

Then we know that since $u(x)$ is a utility function

$$u(x_2) = (\alpha, x_1; 1 - \alpha, x_3)$$

$$= \alpha u(x_1) + (1-\alpha)u(x_3)$$

$$= \alpha, \text{ since } u(x_1) = 1$$

$$u(x_3) = 0$$

We can now join together the Von Neumann and Morganstern axioms for the existence of a utility function and the argument as developed on lottery tickets.

Let us consider a basic reference lottery with winning and losing prizes of W and L. We can now construct a functional relationship of $\phi(x)$ against x where x is a certain monetary equivalent and $\phi(x)$ is the comparable proportion of winning tickets in the basic reference lottery. We observe first of all that the nine axioms all apply to the certain money equivalent x in the basic lottery. Secondly we have seen how any other lottery with prizes in between W and L can be transformed into the basic reference lottery and also, using this transformation, any compound lottery can be transformed into the single basic reference lottery.

Hence, the function $\phi(x)$ is a utility function for the x's and moreover we have seen that the two consequences of the Von Neumann and Morganstern axioms apply as particular cases to the $\phi(x)$ namely

(i) that if $x_1 > x_2$

$$\phi(x_1) > \phi(x_2)$$

and (ii), the breakdown of any lottery with prizes $L\,x\,y\,W$ shows

$$\phi(\alpha, x; 1 - \alpha, y) = \alpha\phi(x) + (1 - \alpha)\phi(y).$$

As has been seen the utility function $\phi(x)$ is not unique. For example, a constant can be added to or multiply the $\phi(x)$ and all the results still apply. We are now able to use these results where the x's refer to incommensurable alternatives. Suppose we have a set of alternative objectives which have the following properties:

(i) We shall obtain one and one only of these alternatives (note—one 'alternative' can be the failure to obtain any of them).

(ii) It is possible to rank the alternatives in an increasing order of attractiveness.

We now state this ranking and consider the basic reference lottery in which the losing prize is the least attractive of these alternatives and the winning prize is the most attractive. As before, in the continuous case, we form for each of the remaining alternatives the indifference probability between having this alternative for certain and partaking in a basic reference lottery with given proportions of winning and losing tickets corresponding to the most favoured and least favoured alternatives.

In this way the utility of any course of action can be calculated. The problem of deterministic response is straightforward, the utilities associated with the different goals can be combined. The problem of probabilistic response can also be dealt with since the property of utilities is that they can be dealt with in terms of statistical expectations.

It must be conceded that utility theory has an attractive elegance associated with it. That being so, we may ask why it is that it is so little used in any real practical case. The reader is enjoined to beware of supposed practical cases where it is claimed that utility theory has been used effectively to take major decisions. Such claims are usually made by the analysts and rarely can one find them endorsed by the decision maker himself.

Why, then, have so many managerial horses refused to drink from the utility water?

Firstly, there is the problem of credibility. Just as decision theory loses credibility when it states that in some cases the optimal course of action for an experienced manager is literally to toss a coin, so it does seem facetious to treat major strategic objectives by inviting those concerned to consider lotteries in which these objectives are to be the prizes.

Secondly, there is the problem of group decision making. As it stands, the theory is essentially for one person's decisions—a group utility cannot exist.

Thirdly, there is the problem of elitism. It takes a clever person to deal in the concepts of the probabilities of events which one knows are not actually going to occur. The questions which have to be asked (and answered) in order to create a utility, involving the alternative of having something for sure or possibly have one or two other things with complementary probabilities, are not of the sort which can be posed to the man in the street with any confidence that one will receive a helpful answer. Some examples, such as deciding on the optimal location of a nuclear power station, can only have utility functions derived by sophisticates and for an answer acceptable to the population at large one might be better advised to go to a (corrupt) politician who will shortly be running for office.

Finally, as is demonstrated in Chapter 12 this method is one which depends on breaking down a complex decision into its separate parts and then, in some way, adding the bits together again. It may be that there is a resentment against destroying the integrity of a total policy in this way.

9 Competitive Problems

'He rejoiceth as a strong man to run a race'
Psalm 19

The area of competition

In all the models which have so far been discussed, we have made the assumption that the variables consist of only two types. There are those variables which are directly under the control of the decision-maker and there are those which are uncontrollable and may be regarded as state of nature variables. However, in competitive situations we are dealing implicitly with problems in which there is a third category of variables, that is those variables which are under the control of a rival. As a general rule it may be assumed that the objective of the rival is such as to be partly contrary to our own objective. This, of course, is not always so and there are many important cases where, although competition may appear to exist, a closer examination will show that competition is in fact not present.

It is certainly the case that in most competitive industry, both in the private and nationalized sectors, there are extensive areas in which cooperation between rival firms will in fact take place. Sometimes this cooperation is in the field of the acquisition of resources. In the oil industry, for example, rival companies which may be in great competition in their marketing effort will co-operate in exchanging drilling and exploration data in those areas where they are assessing the possibility of virgin land being oil-bearing. The reason for this may be an antipathy between the oil companies and the state which is selling or leasing the land. In the face of what they regard as being a greater rival than themselves, the companies will combine. There are other cases where rival companies may combine in production. Sometimes this will take the form of cooperating in research into improved production processes. A great deal of the work of the research associations is concerned with the production process and rival companies will share information. Equally, they will cooperate in negotiating national agreements for labour costs and hence, in an area which determines their total efficiency, they will seek to remove competition for skilled workers. In the marketing field there is not generally so much cooperation, although there do sometimes seem to be implicit arrangements, of an unpublicized form, in which companies will combine to arrange a selling price. They may combine too in the form of the marketing and advertising effort which they are likely to deploy. There is at least one major company which exists to distribute the products of two companies (which jointly own it) while the two companies compete in all other activities, including marketing. In addition, of course, there are many examples of competing brands of product within the same organization.

At first sight it might be thought that most competitive problems arise in the marketing of finished products and indeed most research into competition has originated in this field. On the other hand, of course, those pieces of research which are concerned with the marketing of finished products, may also be applied to the purchasing of raw materials. In this chapter we shall show some of the principles by which models in competitive situations should be developed.

It is a curious feature that for years many operational research scientists have fought shy of carrying out work in the marketing area. Some have felt moral objections to this, and indeed some operational researchers will not carry out any research into the marketing process. There is, in addition, a somewhat old-fashioned snobbery, particularly in Britain, to the effect that although it is perfectly honourable and praiseworthy to buy raw materials, manufacture goods and manipulate finance, there is something rather reprehensible and shameful about actually selling the product; and yet, of course, the marketing area is the one part of an organization which generates income. All other parts of an organization activity are concerned with spending money in some optimal fashion.

The market

One of the first and basic decisions which have to be taken in all marketing problems is to define what the market is. Any parameter which is based on share of market implies information and definition of the products which are in competition with the particular products whose market share we are evaluating. Sometimes this is clear-cut. In other cases it is much less clear. For example, the cinema is clearly in competition with other parts of the entertainment industry, including theatres and night clubs. It is also in competition with the neighbourhood public house? Is it in competition with restaurants or sport? The definition of the market affects the whole of the competitive strategy. Even within a single product the definition of the market may not be straightforward. To take the sales of a particular brand of beer as an example, it is possible to define the market in the following terms:

1. Sales of all beers.

2. Sales of all alcoholic drinks.

3. Sales of all beverages.

4. Sales of all foods.

What is necessary in all these problems is to take the consumers' expendable money and to see the extent to which the money which is devoted to a particular product is at risk, by the sales or opportunities to buy of certain specified other products. It is by doing this that the marketer gains an insight into the total competitive pressure within which he is operating. As has been pointed out elsewhere, however, we must create some boundaries to the problem and there will often not be a natural boundary to the market of a product.

Method of approach

There are many ways in which one can approach so complex and ill-structured an area as that of competition. We could, first of all, take various types of problem in the area of competition and hence cover advertising models, models of consumer expendables and consumer durables, and models of consumer behaviour in a variety of fields, leading on to the field of competitive tendering. Such an approach would be valid and indeed many writers have adopted it. We shall, however, adopt a slightly different approach. We shall take, first of all, an approach by means of formulating simple, logical structures which might be expected to obtain in a competitive situation. We shall examine the implications of these structures, not only in terms of data requirements, but also in terms of implementation. By approaching the problem in this way, we wish to dispose of an approach to marketing problems which is, unfortunately, very prevalent, namely the approach through massive data analysis. It is certainly the case that competitive systems, particularly those in the field of marketing, have the capacity to generate quantities of data which can now be examined in detail by means of massive data processing procedures. As has been seen, in general, we reject the approach to model construction via such statistical analyses. Even when statistical analyses yield an apparent relationship between cause and effect, one is forced at the end of the analysis to explain the relationship in some formal qualitative fashion. It is probably not too strong a comment to insist that in any form of research an immediate appeal to formal regression techniques is a confession by the analyst that either he does not understand what is going on or, alternatively, he is unwilling to invest his own brain power in trying to formulate qualitative hypotheses.

The simplest form of hypotheses in competitive situations arises in the field of advertising. As we have already illustrated in Chapter 4, we can make the assumption that 'all other things being equal' there will be an increasing relationship between the amount of sales of the product and the amount of advertising. This amount of advertising is almost always measured in terms of the total money spent. It is an unhappy relfection on the work of advertising agencies, that whereas most concern in an agency is with the form of message by which the product is announced, that is the pictures and the words which go with the pictures, unfortunately most advertising research which attempts to relate the sales to the advertising expresses the advertising simply in cost.

If we formulate such a model in its most simple form, then we have a functional relationship between the amount of sales and the amount of advertising in which the sales monotonically increase with advertising. Such a functional relationship leads to two questions. The first is the extent to which sales will exist in the absence of advertising, and the second is where lies the upper bound?

If the relationship of sales to advertising has this upper bound, and it is difficult to conceive of situations where it does not, then we will expect an asymptotic approach to this upper limit, of the form shown in Figure 39.

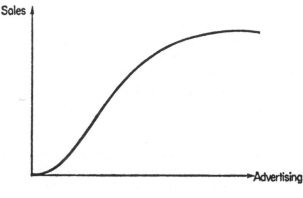

Figure 39

There are a variety of functions which will give such a relationship. In all these relationships the two basic variables are the rate at which sales increase with advertising at any level of advertising, and the upper limit. The former of these is important, because in any process of allocating a total expenditure between different amounts of advertising, it is the slope of the curve at any point which gives an important necessary condition for an optimal allocation.

In stating the amount of advertising, we have omitted another important feature, namely the period over which advertising is assumed to have an effect. This is where one has to be careful not to be confused by accounting conventions. It is convenient, for example, in many cases to assume that the effect of advertising is deployed over the accounting period of the organization. If advertisements are paid for during, say, a four-week period, it then becomes convenient to relate sales to the amount of advertising in that four-week period. This is one of the insidious dangers of using accounting data, and indeed some advertising models explicitly use a given period as the time over which advertising is assumed to have an effect, simply because of the accounting base.

In determining the effect of advertising at any time, one has to accumulate the effect of advertising over the past periods. In some models this weight of advertising is simply an average figure over the last six weeks or whatever the time may be. This then gives a constant weight to all advertising over a fixed time period. Other models take some form of smoothed advertising weight. Exponential smoothing, for example, may be used and in this case, of course, all past advertising is assumed to make a contribution in terms of today's weight. In practice, of course, such past advertising has very little effect in terms of today's total advertising weight. The third factor which applies in these models is the discount or decay factor to be applied to past advertising. This will be a function which is related to the time which has elapsed since the advertisement was shown. The use of such functions enables one to derive a net accumulated weight of advertising at any present time. To sum up, in these models we have the three basic variables which we must estimate. The first is the form of the function which relates some parameter of advertising to sales. The second is the bound of this function and the third is the parameter which is used as the controllable variable in the model.

One must also be clear what it is one is measuring. In some cases the models are related to the share of advertising rather than an absolute figure for advertising. This in turn is related to the share of market which the product obtains rather than the absolute figure of sales. Hence when the share of market figure is used, one faces a difficult task in stating a bound, although we might, for example, form an understanding of the absolute upper limit for sales of a product in terms of the market saturation.

Such models as these will all depend on either a fortunate conjunction of the availability of adequate quantititative data or, as is more likely, they will need the setting up of a series of experiments in order that the main parameters in the model can be deduced. It is beyond the scope of this book to outline forms of experiments, but one important remark can be made. In many situations where there is very little knowledge or understanding about the total marketing model, it is tempting to try to answer quickly a series of specific questions, which have been posed because of a crisis. It must be strongly emphasized that such temptations should be resisted. While it may be necessary to answer crisis questions by a series of *ad hoc* investigations, the best form of research expenditure in the face of lack of knowledge, is to formulate a series of experiments which will be mutually supporting in their results, in such a way that one can create a fabric of knowledge. This will not generally stem from answering crisis questions, in a crisis manner, by rapid investigations. If one wishes to formulate a total model for a merketing activity, it is necessary to take time and to formulate a hypothetical macromodel, and from this to deduce separate functional relationships by means of special experiments.

Heterogeneous response

So far we have attempted to show, in this simplistic approach to advertising, the way in which one might adduce certain functional relationships as a form of working hypothesis. It cannot be too strongly emphasized, however, that the form of these hypotheses is not very clear. There are cases (we have referred to one in Chapter 4) in which the basic logic which might be assumed to exist will no longer exist. Hence we must be careful when formulating experiments, to make them of a type in which one is not only estimating parameters in the functional equations, but also testing the basic hypothesis regarding the functional equation itself.

In this argument, we have assumed that the total market of custsomers for a product is homogeneous and will have the same functional relationship to advertising weight. In some cases, there is evidence to show that such functional relationships cannot be regarded as applying to all members of the market. It is a useful first working rule to try to fix such functional relationships on the simplest of all null hypotheses, namely homogeneity and consistency of the market. But if the functional relationship cannot be fitted in the form which is posed by the null hypothesis, the next stage should be to examine the assumption of the homogeneity of the market and to see whether it should be divided into sub-categories. In this area, the normal methods of design of experiments, as formulated in standard stastical theory, become important.

Other forms of modelling take this breakdown of the total market population to its extreme by considering the effect of advertising on individuals. It is appropriate at this stage to introduce the concept of brand loyalty. If advertising one particular product has the effect of increasing sales, then the effect of this is to increase all the sales of all products in that particular market and/or it will increase the sales of the product in question at the expense of its rival products. If this is the case then we have persuaded some persons who would normally have bought a rival to switch to our own product. Although determination to buy the same brand is an intuitive concept it is difficult to express in a formal sense what is meant by such brand loyalty. For example, Rao[19] treats brand loyalty by considering a market where there are K brands in a product class. If a consumer has no brand preference, then we can compare his purchasing process to a simple random sampling process, in which the universe is the set of all packages of each brand. In the long run the individual will satisfy a proportion $\frac{1}{K}$ of his requirements from each brand. Thus the minimum possible value of the proportion, p, of his expenditure on his favourite brand will be $\frac{1}{K}$, and as this proportion increases so his loyalty increases. Rao, therefore, proposes the measure of partiality $B = \frac{p-1/K}{1-1/K}$ and converts this to a brand loyalty index $Z = \frac{BL}{100}$, where L is the time over which this brand has been his favourite. However defining brand loyalty may be a more difficult task than it appears. Suppose a consumer buys two competing products regularly and buys no other than these. In odd months one is bought and even months the other. Is the consumer brand loyal?

If we can derive loyalty indices, we may, therefore, estimate the effect of an advertising campaign in terms of its effect on the population of loyalty indices for that particular product. Suppose the effect of such a campaign in terms of its effect on the brand loyalty figures could be deduced, it would then be the case that the mean and possibly the variance of the distribution of these brand loyalty indices in the population would be altered. The usual Markov approach can then be used to show the ultimate effect on market share of an advertising campaign, by taking the transition probabilities of a consumer moving from the ith product in period n to the jth product in period $(n+1)$. There have been many attempts to use a Markov formulation to estimate the total effect of the future of an advertising campaign. Sometimes this is used to show the way in which advertising should be pulsed over a period of time, to give a maximum effect on sales. There are interesting mathematical formulations which one can make in terms of the way in which a total amount of advertising should be spread out over a total period so as to make its maximum effect (however effect is measured) either in terms of the macromodel relating sales to advertising as posed earlier or in terms of some form of switching of brand loyalties, approached through a Markov process. Although many attempts have been made to formulate consumer models in terms of brand switching, to date there has not been a great deal of success achieved from such modelling.

Quality of advertising

The effect of the quality of advertising is one which is difficult, indeed almost impossible to evaluate at present. Some experiments have been carried out in which groups of consumers are isolated and shown advertisements as part of a general entertainment programme. Questions are put to them before and after the programme as an attempt to evaluate the effectiveness of the advertisements. Such experiments as these assume that there is no change in the decay factor. In addition, highlighting advertisements by setting artificial experiments might be assumed to affect in some way or other, as yet unknown, the choice of hypothetical consumers.

Other attempts relate the number of people who can recall the advertisement in question after a given lapse in time. In these cases one is forced into making a number of assumptions for which justification is not obvious. Some models depend on the number of people who have seen an advertisement in a given period of time. Many models of television advertising are of this nature. The period of time over which the advertisements have been seen and also the requirement as to the minimum number of times the advertisement has to be seen to be effective, are both constraints on the form of model. It is, for instance, possible to formulate advertising schedules on television which will maximize the number of people in a four-week period who have seen a particular advertisement at least three times. The relationship of the four weeks and the three times to actual sales is rarely formally established. Other attempts to assume a quality index for advertising are related to recall. One is concerned here with, for example, maximizing the number of people who can remember a particular advertisement two weeks, three weeks or four weeks later. While it may be thought to give some functional relationship of the decay factor to which we referred earlier, it is not necessarily the case that what is remembered about an advertisement is something that will actually cause a sale to take place. There is some evidence that those who buy food for pets are disturbed to see advertisements in which animals and children both appear, the reason apparently being that there is a sub-conscious fear that the animal will attack the child. Such an advertisement may be recalled with great facility because of the fear which it has induced in the observer, and that fear may inhibit the sale of the product.

As will have been noticed, all these descriptions measure the advertising input either in terms of money expenditure or (which will reduce to the same thing) the media allocation. Advertising agencies however, spend most time and research on the content of the advertisement, a qualitative consideration that has not yet been used in the input of advertising models. This area of advertising models, in this most simple sense, where one has not introduced any measure of product quality or promotional expenditure, is still an area in which the difficulty of dealing even with the simplest concepts is such as to make one rather nervous about the possibility of dealing successfully with much more complex and realistic situations.

We must also exercise care, if not extreme scepticism of models which do not include sales as a dependent variable. Models which substitute exposure, impacts, numbers of viewers or memory of the advertisement and use these as implicit indicators of sales may well be maximizing some factor which has little or no relationship with sales. People spend money on advertising in order to increase the contribution to profits from sales; this must never be forgotten in creating advertising models.

Promotional activity

Promotional activity, which is the inducement to buy a product, consists generally of two forms. There are those inducements that are aimed at the actual purchaser of the product, that is the customer, and there are those which are aimed at the ultimate consumer. Sometimes the customer is the consumer but in most marketing the customer is a wholesaler, and the consumer is the ultimate destination of the product in question. In modern marketing, with larger chains of stores, the 'wholesaler' may be a tied supplier to a chain.

The effect of premiums and special offers and also the effect of price on sales, are two areas in which the only way at present to formulate any understanding of the effectiveness of these controllable variables, is to set up special experiments. On premiums (and offers) the experiments have to take account not only of the premiums on the product in question, but also of the competing premiums which may be offered with competing goods. The effectiveness of particular premiums may often be seen, but one is very rarely able to forecast it. Experiments have been carried out in the negative sense, by stopping premiums in particular parts of the country for a period of time in order to observe the effect. This is a dangerous kind of experiment, because it is specifically aimed at causing a loss in sales and hence there will be a considerable cost involved if the experiment is successful. In addition, even though experiments may fail to show a positive effect of premiums, there will be reluctance to stop premiums because of the high cost involved in having made an error in deduction. Consequently, premiums may continue, not because it is necessarily thought that they add something to sales, but because of concern as to the effect of stopping them.

The effect of price on sales is also one in which it is dangerous to assume too readily that one has a simple monotonic function. The reader will be aware of those cases in which the customer has assumed that something which is of a higher price is necessarily of a higher quality, and some pre-testing of products has shown that the same product offered a lower price will achieve lower sales, because the customer assumes that it must be of poor quality.

Media allocation

One important facet of research into advertising is that of media allocation. In many cases one is concerned with making the advertisement available to a certain profile of population, where the profile might be measured in terms of income, social class or particular purchasing habits. Each medium which can carry the advertisement, whether it is a particular television station at a particular time or a particular newspaper or magazine, will have a profile of viewers and readers classified according to the category which is of interest to the advertiser. There are some interesting mathematical formulations which can be deduced for optimizing in some way the total viewing of a series of advertisements in different media. Such formulations, while attractive mathematically (and there are a number of linear programming formulations), all suffer from the same difficulty of formulating properly the objective function. The objective function in marketing is surely some function of sales. Most objective functions in media allocation, however, are at a higher level. They will be functional relationships showing the number of people who have seen an advertisement a given number of times, or the number of people who recall an advertisement or alternatively the number of people in an experiment who satisfy some test with regard to the experiment. All are taken as forms of objectives and yet, of course, the relationship between all these various parameters and actual sales remains to be established. One is consequently forced to try to maximize in some way a function which is not necessarily related to the overall total objective.

The assumption in this argument has been that the consumer of the product is in a certain prior state before being subjected to a stream of advertising. The problem, therefore, is to obtain some measured formulation of this prior state which may be regarded in terms of a pre-purchase disposition. An interesting paper by Emshoff and Mercer[20] formulates a method of stating the relative pre-purchase disposition of the consumer for a number of rival products, discusses the ability of the product to satisfy the needs of the consumer and finally derives a relationship between the consumer's disposition and the brand's ability to satisfy the consumer's needs. This model then derives a conditional probability that a particular customer buys a particular brand in terms of the preferences and the characteristics of the brand.

A model formulation

All these various relationships of the customer to the total marketing strategy are summed up in Figure 40 which presents a logical flow chart of possible relations between cause and effect in a marketing context.

In Figure 40 the central characteristic is an individual customer who loops round in a cycle of product purchase, product use, exposure to outside influences. The influences on the customer represent expenditure by the marketer, while the behaviour of the customer represents a potential income to the marketer. Such a model depends for its solution on a quantitative understanding of the relationships which operate whenever there is a confluence of arrows. In addition, the relevance of the model will depend on its structural relationships being correct. This is typical of the type of model which will not yield to a formal mathematical solution, since the feedback loop inhibits such a formulation. But it can be used to map out the qualitative data analysis needed to formulate the relationships.

Product range

In another context[21] Mercer has shown the importance of distribution which appears in Figure 40. He formulated a model which shows the probability of sales being lost in terms of the variety of products which are offered in a shop and the probability that a particular product will be on sale and in stock.

The interesting result of Mercer's studies has been to show that, in terms of retail outlets offering a range of products, although product range is an important function in determining total sales in a store, it is not necessarily the case that when product range is greater than is needed to achieve a given number of sales, then the least selling product should no longer be stocked. What is not apparent in the situations in the first formulation of the logic, is that the first stage in selling to a customer at a retail store must be to get the customer to come into the shop. Mercer's evidence shows that customers may enter a shop because they are enticed by a particular product which is on sale, but having entered the shop they may then switch to buying another product. If this first enticing product is dropped, because it has very low sales, then it may be the case that total sales from the shop will decrease because customers will cease to enter the store.

Other approaches to studying the range of products to be offered ignore this

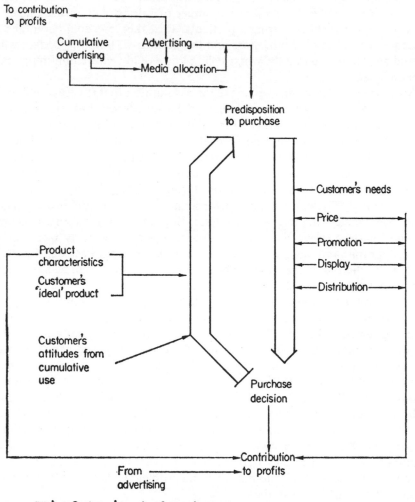

Figure 40. Cause-effect hypothesis in marketing

important conclusion of Mercer. For example, some American work[22] carried out prior to Mercer was aimed at forecasting which particular fashion goods on sale during a limited season were likely to be the ones which sold best. Unfortunately research failed to show in advance of a season which particular items were likely to achieve the highest sales, whether by colour or style. It was possible, however, to use general economic indicators to forecast the total volume of sales which was likely to be achieved during a season. It was also observed that the distribution of sales between the most popular goods and the least popular formed a distribution which was independent of the total volume of sales. If one stated the minimum number of sales which must be achieved for it to be worthwhile offering a particular line, then one could combine the estimate of total sales for the store and the number of lines of product which should be offered, so that the worst selling line would achieve minimum viable economic sales.

An approach such as this will make the assumption that the least selling line has not achieved anything positive, in the way Mercer has indicated may happen. The problem of marketing fashion goods shows how many apparently competitive situations are transformed by the analyst into an allocation problem. This indeed is the most usual transformation which operates in competitive analyses. For example, if a number of different lines of product are offered for sale by a manufacturer during a selling season it will, as has been stated, be difficult for him to formulate prior probability estimates of sales. Nevertheless the increase of sales during the season will often follow a standard pattern in which there is a slow increase in the early weeks of the season, a rapid and maximum rate of sales in the middle weeks and a tailing off towards the end of the season. This rate of increase may well be independent of the total season's sales.

It is possible to use such standard relationships to estimate not only the expected total season's sales of a particular line in terms of the sales achieved by any given period of the season, but also to form a probability distribution of ultimate total season's sales in terms of the sales achieved after any given number of weeks. If such a probability distribution is taken for each line, it can be combined with the contribution to profits (positive or negative) of making and selling (or failing to sell) a unit amount of each line, so as to indicate which of all the lines will give the maximum expected contribution to profit of the manufacture of a single unit of it. Hence it is possible to load up the total production capacity so as to maximize the expected profit from the manufacture. This assumes that all lines make the same demand on the production process. If they do not, then the problem is that of a programming form with non-linear constraints.

Competitive tendering

In all the areas of competition which have so far been described, the rivals in the competitive situation are competing for the attention of the consumer in an indirect manner, having to assume a specific individual form of objective function or by having to assume a particular form of the total model. In these cases the direct confrontation of rivals in the competitive situation is lacking. All the rivals are dealing with ill-structured situations in which the abundance of data is not such as to lead to greater clarity of understanding. However, there is one important area of competition in which there is a direct confrontation of rivals in a more clearly structured situation. This is the field of competitive bidding.

Competitive bidding operates not only in the marketing side of a company's activity but also on its purchasing side. In one case the competition is won by those who offer the lowest prices (marketing) and in the other by those who offer the higher prices (in tendering to purchase). The situation as treated by the analyst is identical in both cases. The models which are formulated in bidding are well treated in Mercer.[20] They all have as their first objective an evaluation of the probability that a bid of a given amount for a given property will succeed. These probabilities are generally evaluated in a static form; that is, they take no account of the economic and production situation of the rival bidders. Nor do they take account of any changes in bidding procedure over a period of time. Some of the earliest approaches in this problem are recounted in a paper by Rivett and Hansmann.[23] In this approach an appeal is made to distributions which show the relationship between the amount an organization bids and the value of the thing being offered. The distribution of the ratio of each individual bid to the average of all the bids on that property can be derived. The estimate of the number of competitive bidders and also their average bid, can also be related to the value of the property being offered. Hence, if a number of properties are simultaneously offered for bid it may be possible to derive the probability of a bid of a given amount on a given property succeeding. This formulation of the bidding problem makes the assumption that past history is an adequate guide to formulate a disribution of bids. It also makes the assumption that companies which have been highly successful or highly unsuccessful in bidding in the past will, at any time, have the same bidding objectives, and that hence the value of each of the properties is the same to all rivals.

Such work as this demands that there shall be available a history of bids made by rivals whether those bids are successful or not. In the presence of such data it is usually possible to formulate a bidding model of this first stage type. In the absence of such full information, and this may occur when only the winning bid is declared, it is still possible to formulate a model which will estimate the probability of a bid winning. It is also important to be able to refine such probability forecasts by any additional information which may show the size and nature of a rival bid. For example, if bids in marketing are for supplying a finished product, a company which has been successful in a number of tenders in the past may find that its production capacity is fully committed over a period in which other tenders are being solicited. Such companies may well bid at a higher level than companies whose production capacity is under-committed. Any form of intelligence information which shows the commitment of capacity by different companies will obviously also show a way of formulating and refining the probability distribution of bids that might be submitted.

We now have a relation between the size of a bid on a property of given value and the probability of success. This yields an expected profitability from any given size of bid on each property. Lagrange multipliers may be used to show how a total amount of bids should be allocated between the alternative properties, so as to maximize the expected total profitability. (For an excellent bibliography on competitive bidding see Stark.[24])

Static bidding

This method makes two important assumptions. It makes the assumption that the value of the items being bid for is the same to all the rivals in the bidding competition. It also makes the assumption that the constraint of committing oneself to a fixed total amount to be bid is realistic. This is unrealistic in two ways. First of all one should always examine the change in the total expected return from the optimum allocation of bids as a function of the total amount bid, in order to determine whether this total amount to be bid should be changed. It also makes the assumption that it is realistic to limit bidding to the total amount bid rather than the expectation of total amount to be paid. (Although this argument is in terms of buying, the argument in terms of selling would be exactly the same.)

In this purchasing situation, in order to adjust the constraint to a more realistic form it is necessary to solve the problem by iteration. For any given total amount bid, one can estimate not only the expected amount to be paid in winning bids but also the statistical distribution of this amount, on the assumption that the probability of winning any one particular object is independent of the probability of winning any other. At present there seems to be no formal analytic solution of this and hence the problem is made more realistic by adopting this iterative procedure.

Sometimes this approach is used in a static situation for a particular company. Take the case of a production manager who is asked whether he will accept an order for a given amount of product to be made over a given period of time. There is a danger of two types of error. The profit margin may be set too low. In this case capacity will be committed too soon and ultimately more profitable business than that which he has accepted will be rejected. On the other hand the forward planning of profit margin may be set too high, and the plant will be working at under capacity. A decision as to which minimum profit margin he should take, such that any business which offers a greater margin than this will be accepted and any business which offers a lower margin rejected, is one which can be formulated and solved in an elegant manner. The flow of cause and effect in this situation is as shown in Figure 41.

In order to maximize the profitability at which orders are booked into the plant, we need the probability distribution of the profits of orders which are currently being offered in the market. Such a probability distsribution is most usefully expressed in terms of profitability per machine each week of each of the orders which are on offer. The forecast of forward spare capacity is obtained from the order book (see Figure 42).

Such relationships, in which rapid decline suggests ultimate under-capacity of working, can lead to quantitative forecasts of the level of capacity at which

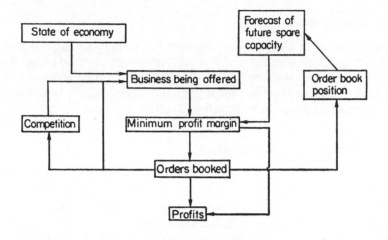

Figure 41

the plant will be operating in any future period if business stays at its same level and the minimum profit margins apply. The distribution of profits per machine week of the orders on offer, can then be used to show how the minimum profit margin should be changed so as to bring in (or exclude) the correct amount of business for the plant to be working to capacity in any future period.

Such functions as these are most important in determining solutions to problems. At the very least they offer the possibility that if mistakes are made either in logic or arithmetic, then these mistakes will be self-correcting; that is, there is a negative feedback from error and hence the system is stable.

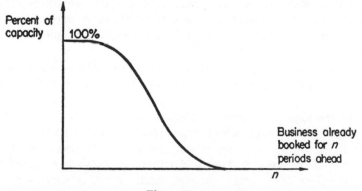

Figure 42

Games and hypergames

We have referred in Chapter 2 to the need to understand the other person's world view and his objectives. This is particularly so in those cases which are structured and dealt with by a game theoretic approach. Where there is no mutuality of objective by the competitors and where there is latent instability the understanding of conflict analysis is essential.

Level of approach in conflict problems

A crucial factor in dealing with conflict situations is the level of the views held of the other parties involved. As with modelling in many other fields, there is a balance to be made between the demands of complexity—on the one hand, and simplicity—on the other, when selecting a model.

One way of classifying the possible levels of analysis is shown in Table 8. Here, the varoius alternatives, ranging upward from totally ignoring the other parties, are arranged in a hierarchy of conceptual complexity and, by implication, use of decision-making 'resources'.[25] In the simplest 'non-interactive' types of model, the other parties are not regarded as purposive actors in their own right. Instead, they are either totally ignored (1) or viewed essentially as passive components of 'nature' (2). This corresponds to the dichotomy suggested earlier in this chapter. In the second region, the other parties are credited with some individuality but are assumed to hold views of the world that are the same as one's own. Models in this region range from the simplest, when the basic idea of rule-observing behaviour first enters the picture (3), through stereotypes (4) to a view in which the other parties are assumed to be like ourselves (5), and then to the highest level in this region (6), where they may be seen to have complex individual personalities and aims. But they are still assumed to share our own view of the situation in which we are involved.

Only in the third, most sophisticated region is this last constraint abandoned. It is now supposed that each party may have his own view of the situation (7). Furthermore, each may have his own view *of the other parties* (8): especially, we allow that each will form his own appreciation of *our own aims and objectives*.

We also note that in many situations it may be helpful to work with *multiple alternative models*, which can be tested against each other as decision-making proceeds.

Clearly, the level of model used can profoundly affect the decision-making process.[26] It has been convincingly argued that there are strong pressures to use oversimplified models, particularly in conditions of crisis, when decision-makers are under stress.[27] The rigid adherence to such a model may well account for many of the often quite spectacular errors of judgement commonly associated with these conditions.[28]

Table 8

Table of models used of other parties in conflicts (after Sharp)

View of other party	Appropriate form of analysis
1. Totally ignored 2. Incorporated passively into 'nature'	Non-interactive region: gambling theory, etc.
3. Machine-like model 4. Simple man-like model 5. Like ourselves 6. As entity in own right, though with similar world-view to our own	Game theory, etc.
7. As entity in own right, with own definition of situation 8. As entity in own right, with own definition of situation including specific model of ourselves	Hypergame theory

Implications for formal analysis

As we have seen, the framework usually used to model problems involving conflicts of interest is that provided by *Game theory*. Game theory is normally applied on the assumption that the players are well-informed as to the game being played, i.e. of each other's preferences and strategies. Though their interests may diverge, they thus have a common perception of the problem in hand. But in real life—and even in some simple 'laboratory games'—it is clear that decision-makers' perceptions of the situation may differ radically. We thus need a model lying in the third, rather than the second, region of the hierarchy described above. In effect, the players are trying to play different games: one cannot satisfactorily describe the interaction using a single game.

One way of extending and generalising the Game-theoretic framework to deal with such situations is to use the idea of a *Hypergame*.[29] Roughly, this is a system composed of a 'stack' of perceptual games, one for each player. Any action by one player will be interpreted by each of the others within the context of his own perceptual game. (This is by no means the only approach to generalising Game theory: for example, Harsanyi[30] considers 'games with incomplete information' in which players have probabilistic knowledge of each other's strategies and utilities.)

For comparison, we give formal definitions of a Game and a Hypergame. For the sake of generality, we assign preference orderings for the players rather than the utility scales of the original Von Neumann and Morgenstern treatment.

An *n-person Game* in normal form is a system consisting of:

G.1: a set P_n, of n elements, interpreted as the *players* of the game,

G.2: for each $p \; \varepsilon \; P_n$, a non-empty finite set Sp, interpreted as the set of *strategies* available to p,

G.3: for each $p \; \varepsilon \; P_n$, an ordering relationship Op, defined over the product space $S_1 x \dots x \; S_n$. This is interpreted as *the ordering of player p's preferences* over the set of possible outcomes of the game. We may assume partial or complete ordering.

Each player tries to obtain an outcome as highly preferred as possible, choosing a strategy in the full knowledge of the game though unaware of the specific choices of the other players.

An *n-person Hypergame* in normal form is a system consisting of:

H.1: a set P_n, of n elements (the players of the hypergame),

H.2: for each $p, q \; \varepsilon \; P_n$, a non-empty finite set S_p^q

H.3: for each $p, q \; \varepsilon \; P_n$, an ordering relationship O_p^q defined over the product space $S_1^q x \dots x \, S_n^q$.

S_p^q and O_p^q are interpreted, respectively, as *the set of strategies available for p, and p's preference ordering, as perceived by q*. That is, they express q's view of p's options and aims. The sets $S_1^q, S_2^q \dots , S_n^q$ make up q's strategy matrix, and with the set P_n and the orderings O_1^q, O_n^q comprise *q's game* within the hypergame, denoted G^q. The hypergame can thus be considered as the set of n games $G^1, \dots , G^n$.

We define an *outcome of the hypergame* as a strategy n-tuple $\langle s_1^1, s_2^2, \dots , s_n^n \rangle$, where in general s_p^p denotes an element of the set S_p^p. That is, each player chooses from his self-asigned strategy set. This may or may not appear as an outcome of a given player's game. We can thus see that hypergame players—unlike players in an idealised game—may be subject to strategic surprise. That is, another player may have a strategy that one had not bargained for, so that a completely unexpected result can obtain. A hypergame case-study of just such a situation—namely the fall of France in 1940—has been published.[31]

As before, each player tries to obtain the most highly preferred outcome he can. He must choose a strategy appearing in his own game, and he has full knowledge of this game. Regarding information *about the rest of the hypergame*, however, various possibilities arise. A player may have knowledge *only* of his own game, which he assumes is being played by all. Or he may realise that the other parties' perceptions of the situation may differ from his own: he may then have more or less of an idea of what games these other players are trying to play (i.e. he may have 'cross-game' information). Once these information conditions are specified, we may extend the various Game-theoretic criteria of choice and of stability of outcomes to hypergames. There is not space to discuss this in detail. Instead, we illustrate the general idea of Hypergame Analysis by means of an example. For simplicity, we use a two-person case in which each player sees only his own game.

Suppose our 'players' (p,q) are the rulers of two nations. Each desires peace but is suspicious of the intentions of the other. Such a situation forms the basis of a well-known cautionary tale.[32] A search for 'security' prompts an arms race, in which ones own weapons are seen as purely defensive while those of 'the other side' are clearly offensive. The story ends with a 'mad rush on both sides to the launching platforms', as each side tried to pre-empt the other's expected attack.

Now, we can give a hypergame model of this situation that is a rather compelling alternative to the usual game-theoretic ones. Suppose that, at any given stage in the story, each decision-maker has a straight choice between a co-operative strategy (C) and an aggressive one (A). Both perceive this to be the case: their perceptual games have the same strategy matrices. (This restricted form of hypergame is similar to the 'm-game' idea discussed briefly by Luce and Adams.[33]) Player p, we suppose, places the four possible outcomes in the following order of decreasing preference:

$<C, C>$ 'Peaceful co-existence'
$<A, C>$ 'Attack without q retaliating'
$<A, A>$ 'Mutual aggression'
$<C, A>$ 'Suffer attack by q without replying'

Alas, these preferences are not correctly perceived by q. q imagines p to have the following preference order:

$<A, C>$ 'Attack and get away with it'
$<C, C>$
$<A, A>$
$<C, A>$

Similarly, with the roles of the players reversed. Each really wants only to counter the imagined aggressive tendencies of the other. This 2-person hypergame can be represented by the double matrix shown in Figure 43.

Looking at the situation from p's point of view, i.e. at the game G^p, it will be seen that q has a dominant strategy—A. So, p may reason, he must act on the assumption that q will adopt this aggressive strategy. He, p, is faced then with a choice between outcomes $<C, A>$ and $<A, A>$. Of these, the latter is more preferred. So it seems only rational to be aggressive also. The argument for q, looking at G^q is quite analogous. The important point here is that we can analyse, in a systematic way, the effects—here crucial—of the players' differing perceptions. This cannot be done using a single game to describe what is happening. In the game that would be being played if the players had not mistaken each others' preferences, neither would be tempted to deviate from cooperation. The game that would be being played if each player's preferences *really* were ordered in the more aggressive way assumed above by the other turns out to be the well-known 'Prisoners' Dilemma'. This game—

usually used to model this problem—does give a 'rationale' for the 'dash to the launching-platforms'. But then the essential element of the story — mis-understanding — is left out. Our players' preferences are *not* ordered as in the 'P.D.' game, *but each thinks the other's are*. Each 'country' is trying only to defend itself against an imagined threat, and would like nothing better than peaceful co-existence. To what extent this turns out to be an accurate representation of any real-world conflict, is, of course, another question. From the point of view of the 'players' in a complex conflict, a technique such as hypergame analysis can be of practical help in aiding the construction and testing of alternative models. That is, one can start to explore in a systematic way what perceptions might lead to what observed behaviour by the other parties. There is then less chance that one's decisions will be based on assumptions that forever escape critical examination.

Hypergame showing perceptions of hostility

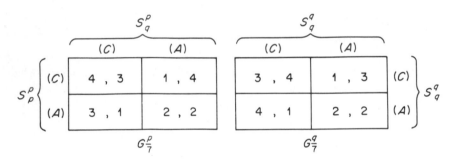

(Figures represent ordinal preferences, with more preferred outcomes assigned higher numbers)

Related games...

No misperceptions

4 , 4	1 , 3
3 , 1	2 , 2

'Prisoners' Dilemma' game

3 , 3	1 , 4
4 , 1	2 , 2

Figure 43

Summary

What can one say in general about competitive problems? Firstly, be careful of the objective function. It may not be that of the organization as a whole. It may have been formulated solely for reasons of model construction and solution, where the model itself is unreal but solvable. Secondly, wherever possible take time to understand. Avoid massive data analysis; apply data collection and analysis to the critical points of a formal hypothesis. Thirdly implement carefully. Competitive problems exist in a fluid environment. Finally, build up a fabric of mutually supporting research. Do not be content with urgent *ad hoc* studies.

10 The Problem of Forecasting

'Forecasting is very difficult, especially when it concerns the future'
Anon.

AS HAS been seen earlier the model and the objective function both consist of a mixture of variables which are controllable and uncontrollable. We have also pointed out that there is a shading of controllability.

One of the problems of dealing with uncontrollable variables, both in the model and in the objective function, is that of devising forecasts for them. In some cases these forecasts are derived in terms of point estimates about which we may by some Bayesian approach, form a probability distribution. These are the *static* variables, within the terms of which we solve the model against the objective function. We can regard them as being constant over time. For example, in linear programming we may well have to estimate a number of such static variables and introduction of probability in this level is simply in order to test the solution of the linear programme for sensitivity.

There are, however, other categories of uncontrollable variables where we are concerned with a series of point estimates over a period of time, such as for example a time series. In these cases we are generally provided with historical data, say commodity prices, from which the task is to try to forecast the value of the variable at specific instants or over a period of time.

The easiest approach to this problem is the simplistic one which is very tempting to the statistician, namely to assume that nobody knows anything about the structure and that what one has to do is to take numbers and analyse them for underlying structure. The basic problem divides into what are loosely called 'the long term' and 'the short term' forecasting problems. In the long term forecasting problem (and it must be emphasized that long term and short term are purely relative concepts) we analyse the series for the two basic components of trend and cycle. By trend we mean the liability of the long term moving average to change, and by cycle we mean the property of the series to oscillate about a basic mean given by the trend. In these analyses (which are well written up in Gregg and Coutie[34]) we first extract from the historical data an estimate of trend. This is generally carried out by some form of regression analysis which is linear in nature. If we are concerned with a non-linear trend, we are generally content to estimate it over a long term period by means of a series of successive straight lines. A short term trend of a non-linear nature can be approximated to as some form of cyclic effect. Having then, by means of regression analysis, extracted from the data any basic trend, the residual historical variations from this trend are analysed for cyclic effects. There are many methods of dealing with this problem.[34, 35]

Generally one is content to extract trend and cycle, and, having done so the residual variations about the combined trend and cycle are analysed on an historical basis for short term variations. What now happens is that in forecasting one extrapolates forward the trend and cycle and the divergence from this trend and cycle is taken as a residual variation from the mean of a distribution. Here then the problem in short term forecasting is based on the hypothesis that we have now a static situation in which the variables with which we are dealing can be regarded as independent samples from some statistical distribution, whose mean is given at any moment by the combination of trend and cycle. Once again there are many methods of dealing with this. One can estimate the mean of this distribution from the moving average of the residual variations over a period of time into the past. Alternatively one may recognize that more weight may be given to recent variations from the mean than past variations, and develop some form of exponentially weighted moving average. For these methods standard computer programs are available.

So far we have been dealing with the problem of one single variable in a time series. It may be the case, however, that two separate variables are linked by some means of lag relationship. For example, the sales of a particular product in one country at a moment of time may be shown to be related to the sales of another product in another country at a later moment in time. Here one has introduced the idea of a lag-related variable and these methods have been documented in a fascinating manner in a paper by Coen and others.[36]

Reference has already been made to the provision of computer programs for analysing such series of related data. This presents the operational research scientist with an awkward dilemma. It will be understood that the underlying theme of this book is the necessity to start model construction from a hypothesis which is explanatory in nature, and from this to deduce logically those features which are going to be helpful in decision-making. The temptation is that because one is provided with easy data processing procedures for correlation and the analysis of correlated data, then one should simply take the historical tapes of data and subject them to a whole series of eseentially random tests of association. In doing this it may well be that certain factors of trend or cycle, or of relations with a lag-variable, may be thrown up by the analysis. It may, in fact, be much quicker to analyse rapidly a whole batch of data in what may be termed a random meaningless manner and to derive significant relationships, than to go through the laborious process of understanding the real situation and formulating hypotheses which represent it.

We suggest that, notwithstanding the seductive ease of data analysis, one should nevertheless only carry out such unthinking analyses when one is resigned to the fact that it may be too difficult to formulate a prior hypothesis. The reason is that even when we have, by the unthinking approach, derived a basic 'model' (it will be noted that this is hardly a model at all within the terms used in this book) one still has the task of explaining. Basic to our craft of decision analysis is the need to explain relationships. (It is the task of the executive to manipulate systems which he does not understand and it is the task of the management scientist to try to understand the system.) Consequently we emphasize the need to start, wherever possible, from a basic structure which we induce before any analysis is undertaken. This means, for example, that in estimating cycle and trend we will induce these processes and then test whether what we have achieved is significant. In the same way, in studying the relationship between certain variables we should seek to start with the logical relationship which can be explained, and then to test.

Another method of forecasting is to form a hypothesis whereby the variable which is being forecast can be shown logically to derive from the conjunction of a number of subsidiary variables. The relationships between these subsidiary variables may be adduceable and the individual variables themselves may be subject to some form of control. In this case, what is apparently an uncontrollable random variable may be partly controllable and it may be possible to forecast one partly, by means of the conjunctive structure. An example of this is the study which Ackoff carried out on forecasting sales of a particular brand of beer over a period of time.[7] In summary form, the equation which Ackoff suggested is:

Sales of brand = (Total population)

     × (Proportion of potential beer drinkers)
     × (Average net disposable income per capita)
     × (Proportion of n.d.i. spent on food)
     × (Proportion of food expenditure spent on beverages)
     × (Proportion of beverages which are alcoholic)
     × (Proportion of alcohol which is beer)
     × (Proportion of beer which is brand in question).

As can be seen, the multiplying factors above are partly controllable and partly uncontrollable. In addition the sensitivity of the result to the multiplying factors is such that the less one can control, the greater the sensitivity of the factor. For example, if one could do anything to increase the sales of a particular brand of beer in this situation the logical deduction is that one should try to increase the population. There is, however, a limited amount that one man can do in this situation. Consequently the management scientist will tend to concentrate his attention on the less sensitive but more controllable features. In fact, there is an interesting problem of comparing sensitivity and controllability and seeing where the focus of management's attention should be made.

There remain two important questions which have to be answered in every forecasting problem. The first is the question of the accuracy of forecasts and the second is the question of how far ahead one should attempt to forecast. In considering the accuracy with which we must derive a forecast, we have to remember that the only thing that is certain about any forecast is that it will be wrong. The question at issue is how wrong can we afford to be? Hence whenever forecasts are suggested and incorporated into a model one should test the solution of the model for sensitivity against the errors in forecast. These errors in the forecast will stem from two causes. There will be errors stemming from the fact that we have stated the value of a variable which will be wrong, and there are the errors which stem from the basic distributions which we have assumed. For example, in a dynamic programming problem where we consider a series of variables over a period of time, each of which has its own static distribution appropriate to that particular time, we will have to examine the consequences of assuming these variables to be distributed normally, in a triangular fashion or in a rectangular fashion. In some cases it may well be that the optimal answer to the problem will remain the same even though the form of the distributions are taken to be quite different.

In analysing the relevance of a forecast we need first the effect on errors in the prior distributions that have been used, and secondly, the effect on the consequence of the decision, of errors in the forecast themselves. There are two approaches by which this can be done. One can take the forecasts which are derived and see what the effect is on the optimal course of action, of errors in this forecast, how robust the course of action is to errors in the forecast or changes in the basic distributions. This gives an estimate of how much we should be committed to a particular course of action, which may be regarded in some way as optimal. The second approach is to take a given course of action and study how the pay-off stemming from it is likely to change against errors in the inputs and forecasts. Both of these approaches should be tried before any decisions are made as to any specific course of action which should be followed. For example if, in deriving an optimal solution in a linear programming problem we have made forecasts of certain variables, this approach would mean two sorts of test. One would be to take the optimal course of action as given by the linear program, and to see how the pay-off from it varies as the input parameters are allowed to vary. The second is to take the optimal course of action and examine how much the input parameters have to vary for this course of action to be non-optimal and to estimate the loss in pay-off which will occur because the new optimal course of action is no longer taken.

The second question is how far ahead one should forecast. This naturally links with the problem of the accuracy of forecasting but there is one important difference. Analogies are dangerous things but if we may take one, consider the case that an ocean liner cannot be stopped or have its course significantly changed within the next ten miles. It is, then, at the very least, prudent to be able to see at least ten miles ahead. Consequently, when we consider the period ahead for which we should forecast, we have to ask two questions. The first of these is over what period of time are the actions which we are now taking going to have an effect? Second, to what extent can we change decisions which have already been taken? In consequence of this, in the heavy expenditure for providing energy, such as in building a nuclear power station or in building a new mine, because the investment is going to pay off over a period of twenty to forty years one has to forecast twenty to forty years ahead. In other situations where one has a very fluid, flexible decision-making problem, where it is possible to change one's mind and not be committed far ahead, then one works to a much shorter time period. We can observe the effects of this politically in that it is rare for a government which is going to face a general election, at the maximum of five years ahead to plan for more than five years ahead. It will always seek to extract what credit it can from current situations by means of short term planning and short term forecasts.

Perhaps one can conclude this section with a cautionary tale. Reference has been made above to the problem of forecasting energy consumption. Some years ago the author was concerned with a problem which arose in the mining industry. For many years after World War II the marketing problem of the National Coal Board was simple. One had only to allocate coal to eager custsomers. In the mid-1950s, for the first time, it became difficult to sell small-sized coal, this being the coal which is always the least attractive to the customer and the most difficult to sell. The response to this situation was a considerable research and development plan aimed at producing more large-sized coal. What was not seen at that time was that the increasing difficulty of selling small coal was a symptom of the future difficulty of selling coal itself. The problem was treated as one of product mix and not of total sales. Consequently in the mid-1950s one was forecasting coal sales for the mid-1970s of the order of 320,000,000 tons a year whereas currently (1979) the industry is struggling to maintain sales of only half this amount. The cautionary note is not that the forecasters and planners were incompetent, but that there was the very human error of seeing in a situation what one wants to see. It is always a temptation in forecasting, to be optimistic. Industries, governments, institutions of all kinds, in surveying the future will generally tend to see what they want to see and the human error into which we fell, in the National Coal Board in the 1950s, is not uncommon.

The most secure forecasts are based on a number of different approaches. Forecasting will make use of quantitative data, where necessary moderated by judgement and intuition. Economic indicators can be used to forecast up to eight months ahead but their main usefulness is as descriptors of the present state. Periodic surveys of business men are also of only short term value, perhaps having validity up to one year ahead. A horizon of up to three or four years can be obtained for economy forecasts by the analysis of trends and then extrapolating.

Futures forecasting

We have described above what is essentially the short-term forecasting problem, which can be dealt with by extrapolation. But what of longer-term forecasting which cannot be dealt with merely by assuming that the future is continuous from and contiguous with the present? We now move away from quantitatively based forecasts into more speculative and imaginative fields.

There are a number of separate ways of dealing with this problem. An obvious first approach is to attempt to move forward from the present, even beyond the time period for which this is statistically prudent. Divergence mapping (see later) is a method of sequencing over time a set of alternative possibilities and obviously depends on the continuous nature of our world. Another way of building from the present is to use well established structural relationships of different parts of the economy as a basic logic so as to remove some uncertainty. If there is an understanding of the way economic variables affect each other then we can use an input-output table within and between industries and within and between geographical areas, but this has limited use in forecasting largely due to the delay in producing the tables. For example the UK input-output analysis tables of 1973 were based on 1968 data.

Simulation methods are obviously attractive to the O.R. scientist and are well described in a number of sources. It is suggested they have validity for up to 15 years ahead but for the longer term forecasts which are our present concern, we need to break out of the short term constraints of all these methods. The basic approach is to form scenarios which give a qualitative or quantitative description of the world at a particular future item. The scenario describes scene by scene one or more mental images of the future and for the method to be informative it is important that these images be detailed, self-consistent and real.

Early on in every scenario exercise two crucial decisions must be made:

(a) The timescale.
(b) The number of options.

In time, periods up to 15 years are, as stated, better dealt with by simulation and although the number of options may be infinite, the minimum number seems to be three.

The Delphi technique is well known outside O.R. although many practising O.R. Scientists do not appear to have used it. The method evolves forecasts from a group of people but avoids face to face discussion and confrontation in which the strongest personality, or loudest mouth, may dominate. Forecasts are made anonymously, are exchanged and criticised with (one hopes) a gradual movement towards a consensus view. In practice Delphi coordinators might submit questionnaires to the individuals of a group and report back to them (individually) in the form of edited reports and fresh information. From such a series of questions and answers the group and the coordinators move to a series of forecasts, opinions and scenarios. The opinions of the participators can be focussed upon the provision of a series of scenarios stretching into the future.

Another method of producing future scenarios is to reverse the process of Delphi. In this one writes a description of the world as it might be in the year 2000 and then from the perspective of the year 2000 the history of the previous 25 years is written. In this history, which would take us from the known of 1975 to the suggested world of 2000, one can identify critical points of change in the world which lead to the culmination of the particular history described for the year 2000. By analysing such 'historical' documents one gains an understanding of the events which might have to occur for particular scenarios to obtain in reality. Attention can then be focussed on the likelihood of these events occurring and hence on the likelihood of the particular scenario being evolved.

We now move on to the essentially quantitative methods. All these revolve in some way around the methods of simulation which have been mentioned earlier. We have referred to the interconnectivity of the matters which one is dealing with in future developments and these interconnectivities, in the quantitative approaches, are dealt with by means of correlations or stated relationships. For example, in using a cross impact analysis one is concerned with stating the relationships between various events which might occur and the subsequent events which are affected by these causes. Sometimes these relationships are deterministic in nature, rather akin to the input-output table which we discussed earlier. In other cases the occurrence of an event will affect following events in a probabilistic form. In cross impact analysis one states these probabilities and uses a simulation in order to produce various alternative future scenarios. In practice the method is fiendishly complex and complicated because of the combinatorial problems involved.

Divergence mapping is a pictorial approach for moving from the present into the future. It rests upon the assumption that we are most sure about the present situation and that we are going to move into the future along a series of alternative snapshots, all of which are related to each other by time. Diagrammatically the areas on the map are different scenarios where time is taken as moving out from the central origin. One can only move from one scenario to another as a function of time, and these scenarios are adjacent in the mapping. This is a way of relating a series of scenarios and seeing the extent to which the movement over time is plausible. The method is attractive, as indeed is any pictorial method of dealing with these complex forecasting problems.

In summary, it would appear that the main method of producing forecasts in the medium term is by the qualitative discursive methods referred to in the earlier part of this section rather than by the formal mathematical methods.

Economic Forecasts

Economic forecasts of the future are prolific. We shall merely restrict ourselves to a summary of one in particular. In doing so, it is useful to remember that this most detailed and open long term economic forecast by Leicester[37], which was published in 1972, has little or no reference to those magical words 'North Sea Oil'. Such is the way in which new features can arrive quickly on the scene.

The methods used in Leicester's forecast are at the quantitative end of the above summary of techniques but include as conclusions —

1. By 2000 the level of economic activity will be between two and three times current levels (corresponding to growth rate of at least 3.4 per cent).
2. The largest share of growth will go into investment as opposed to consumption and the next largest into social services.
3. Per capita consumption levels will double—people will live in better houses, with 1.5 cars per household, travelling three times as much; their health will be three times as well cared for (in expenditure terms) and individuals will be better educated.

A social implication of this growth is the extent to which the gap between rich and poor nations will be allowed to grow. Martel[38] points out that over the last 100 years the gap between the ratio of the richest 10 per cent and the poorest 10 per cent of nations has widened. At the beginning of the industrial revolution it was 5:1, today it is about 200:1. This gap might be changed by unionization and consequent high wages increasing the attraction of less developed countries in providing pools of cheap labour.

Social forecasting

In this area we are dealing with an ephemeral but pervasive effect. Ephemeral because of the rapidity with which social factors ebb and flow. The rapid increase in the role of women in society will have profound effects but is comparatively fresh. The car is now a social necessity, but even 25 years ago the standard design of a house did not incorporate a garage. Central heating is now as essential as good sanitation, but even 15 years ago it was an optional extra in a new house. Entertainments are ephemeral; no longer is cock fighting (or even boxing) a popular spectator sport. Speedway languishes and tenpin bowling had a life (in the U.K.) of about 10 years. Twenty years ago computers were glamorous and exciting, now Woolworths sell small computers. We seem to be moving towards an earlier retirement age and this, combined with delay of entering employment caused by education and increased life expectancy will mean that less than half our lives will be spent working for a living and so leisure industries will increase in importance.

But there are social constants. One is geography—not only the natural boundaries of rivers and hills but the astonishing permanence of the man-made urban environment. The layout of towns and cities changes very slowly, even the north and east boundaries of Hyde Park follow Roman roads and have existed for 2000 years.

The sizes of communities (in relation to each other) have changed little over the years. In the U.S.A. over the last 30 years the proportion of the population changing residences has remained almost constant at 20 per cent. per annum. In this country, data for Dorset (for example) show that between 1847 and 1936 the distance separating marriage partners did not exceed 19.5 km in 87 per cent of cases and for the country as a whole in the decade 1953 to 1963 the 87 per cent figure was constant for distances up to 16 km.

Technological forecasts

It is always difficult to forecast the direction of scientific development. Scientists in the public domain (for example universities) are jealous of their freedom of research while those in the private sector may be bound by secrecy. Nevertheless we have less excuse for being taken by surprise by technological change since it casts before it a long shadow of basic research, applied research and development.

The literature reveals a number of interesting points. The thrust of inventions in electronics and computing is probably enough well known for any account here to be repetitious. Mathematical modelling of the rate at which a new product substitutes for an old one shows interesting results.

There are dangers, not always recognised in this kind of forecasting, of failing to recognise a re-entrant technology. Thirty years ago the gas industry was written off by all discerning thinking people. The advent of high speed British Rail virtually destroyed the burgeoning short haul air services between London and Manchester and resuscitated rail travel. We now see the rapid resurrection of radio and are even hearing cries for the return of the tramcar to our city streets.

Political factors

The first sentence of a paper by Rose is 'A paper about the role of forecasting in political science cannot be a review of the literature, because there is no literature'. As Rose states, the basic difficulty seems to be intellectual. If an economist talks of economic change the meaning is usually clear and capable of measurement. When a technologist talks of change what he is implying is visible physically. When a sociologist talks of social change the meaning is less clear and less readily subject to quantified measurement but nevertheless ought to refer to a specified model of the social system. But when political scientists talk of political change it can mean anything (for example, a change in the party controlling a local authority), everything (a totalitarian style revolution) or nothing.

The most important obstacle is the infrequency of observational phenomena. Only four people have led the Labour Party in the last 40 years and only eight have led the Conservatives. The circumstances in which they come to power may be fortuitous (the death of Gaitskell and the illness of Macmillan). As Rose points out, where quantified data are provided they achieve their objective by accumulating quantities of data that are economic or social rather than political. For example, the book, *Political Change in Britain* by Butler and Stokes, published in 1969, is misleadingly titled. To analyse the subject it purports to study, the authors would have had to deal with the politics of three decades, three generations or three centuries, rather than, as was the case, with three sample surveys undertaken in a time span or less than thirty-six months.

The last twenty years have seen the emergence of a science of political forecasting. We have seen the growth of polling and studies of the reasons why electoral campaigns have been fought the way they were. However, most of these studies are centred specifically around a General Election. We do not have continuing studies showing the way in which political views are changing within the population, and the reasons for those changes. We have a great deal of detailed study of General Elections themselves but in looking at a continuous process of political change over a period of years, one is really faced with a series of detailed snapshots at election time with very, very little picture of what is happening in between elections.

Most of our forecasts of political change stem then not from quantitative analysis as such, but from forecasts derived as a result of discussions between experts and industrial managers.

The political forecast here is of a continuing increase in power of the E.E.C. It seems to be conceded that such changes are long term and will continue. What is less sure is the extent to which the present moves towards regionalization in Britain are as definite as the moves towards centralization in Europe. It may be that the social changes which we have seen come about by means of the devolution movements, will be ephemeral. However, one's impression from the literature and from the reports which I have read, is that we are, indeed, faced with the continuing move towards local organization.

In the final section of this chapter we draw a parallel between the number of ways in which two tendencies towards corporate decision making and towards individual decision making seem to be progressing simultaneously. On this basis it seems fair to suppose that the movements towards regionalization and devolution in the United Kingdom, will continue.

The incoherent nature of this section is partly a reflection of the literature on which it is based. There is indeed no such literature and there seems no science of political forecasting as such.

Energy forecasts

This is a literature (even a cottage industry) all of its own and has a major share of market in futures literature. It would be naïve to summarize in a few lines but certain points emerge. This is, first of all not only the largest sector of the forecasting industry but also that in which the largest errors have been made. In 1866 Professor W. S. Jevons forecast that within 100 years the demand for British coal would be 2607 million tons a year (in terms of coal *equivalent* in 1966 energy consumption in the U.K. was 298 million tons).

In 1966 U.K. coal production was 176 million tons. The Robinson commission of OECD (1960) stated that no persistent shortage of primary energy was likely by 1975 (correct) but added the incorrect rider that there was no real need to create new sources of energy[39].

What reliance can be placed on long term energy forecasts? Many forecasting exercises are little more than statistical extrapolations which rely on the assumption that past relationships will continue, rather than being based on an appreciation of the possibilities for economic, social and technical change. Nothing seems to be known about long term energy price elasticities or substitution forecasts. The basic data seem of poor quality—reliable time series for energy consumption were rarely published before 1950 and little can be found about relative demands for different types of power. Even the basic assumption that the correlation between economic growth and energy requirements will continue and may have to be examined; for example energy conservation may affect the relationship between these two factors.

The basic reserves of fossil fuels and uranium deposits are not known with any precision. Whereas the literature tends to treat energy as a finite resource within a statistical analysis framework, the size and composition of 'reserves' keep changing; for example, wood, peat, coal and animal power have been steadily replaced by petroleum, which may itself be complemented by new energy sources.

It would be unrealistic to expect technical progress now to come to a halt and too complacent to rely on it and market forces to provide timely and socially desirable solutions to the energy problems of the future. There do seem to be major uncertainties and this leads to two sharply different schools of thought—the 'apocalyptic' and the 'Lord will provide' school. The analyses of apocalyptic school point to an exhaustion of energy reserves, accompanied by strife and wars as nations fight over dwindling supplies, early next century. (The lack of firm knowledge of resources renders dating difficult). The other school points to the historical evidence of replacement of one form of energy by another (muscle, wood, dung, coal, gas, oil, nuclear) and believes that economic forces and substitutions will lead to further supplies which will be sufficient especially when energy conservation becomes socially desirable.

The pervasive social factor

We have referred above to the ephemeral nature of social concerns. These also impregnate the technical, economic and political and inevitably impose a systemic view of the future.

Two examples of this may illustrate the point. Few could have foreseen that the social desirability of the first motor cars produced nearly one hundred years ago would lead to the development of machines which (in the U.S.A.) would kill 50,000 people a year, pollute the air of major cities, dominate the economics of the world, radically affect the political scene over a large area of the world and lead (perhaps) to wars.

Another example of this is from the United Kingdom. A consequence of increasing social aspirations is that more people go into further education. Amongst these are the skilled and intelligent who previously filled jobs such as gas fitters. The resulting shortage of these skilled men is that gas apparatus used in the home might have to be redesigned so that unskilled labour (including the householder) may deal with it, as is the case with simple electrical connections, for example. This example shows links between social, economic and technological factors. Clearly such social attitudes affect economics. Propensity to save is a social affair, as are the attitudes to energy saving (smaller cars) and attitudes to public transport.

A synthesis

All those concerned with forecasting (including the writer and the readers of this book) are statistical freaks and are not average people. They are part of the articulate middle class, dominantly home counties based and their projections of the future stem from their culture and attitudes. This not only affects the answers to the questions posed but also affects the questions themselves. In so far as the act of forecasting is not neutral in its effect, then this particular freak class will have a leverage effect on the future.

Within the wide range of literature studied a number of strands emerge, sometimes explicitly but more often than not implicitly, so far as U.K. 2000 is concerned.

(1) We shall not be involved in a major war (this possibility is hardly mentioned in the literature).
(2) Economic Growth will continue to be a main objective. With a 3 per cent compound growth rate, this implies a doubling of living standards by the year 2000.
(3) Service Industries will grow, particularly health and education.
(4) Geographical layout of towns and cities will change slowly with gradual migration within the U.K.
(5) The gap between rich and poor nations will not narrow.
(6) Women will take up more senior posts formerly occupied by men. The increase in the number of university graduates will lead to an upgrading of the skills of many jobs.
(7) Most important of all—there will be two competing social forces acting on society—a conflict between what makes for efficiency in

technoeconomic terms and what makes for social well being. This may express itself, crudely, in conflict between corporate and individual solutions.

The corporate pressures include

(a) Political control over more aspects of national life from outside the U.K. —Brussels or a European Parliament.
(b)　Large multi-national companies dealing at supra national level with other multi-nationals.
(c)　More and more decisions of a company being taken at the centre (following the ability to centralise data flow) and a consequent loss of power from regions to the centre.
(d)　The political movements towards the corporate state.

Examples of these are or might be
(i)　Direct elections to a European Parliament.
(ii)　Laws to deal with multi-national activities.
(iii)　Loss of power and status of executives in the provinces compared with London.
(iv)　The emergence of trade unions as dominant partners in national planning.
(v)　Large shareholders increasing their blocks of shares at the expense of the individual shareholder.
(vi)　Pressure on the consumer to use public rather than private transport.
(vii)　The raising of funds and of social engineering by means of pay as you earn income tax.
(viii)　National Health Service, larger universities.
(ix)　Municipalities offering housing, e.g. council houses, for rent.

The contrary movements include
(a)　Devolution.
(b)　Do it yourself technological developments.
(c)　Participation in decision making.

Examples of these are
(i)　The relative sudden emergence after years of ineffectiveness, of movements for devolution in Scotland and Wales.
(ii)　The movement away from laundries and laundromats to home laundries, dishwashing machines, frozen meals (replacing, as a convenience, restaurants) mini calculators and mini computers.
(iii)　Attempts at industrial democracy. (The student participation movement started in 1968. The same students are now in their thirties and moving up the management ladder.)

(iv) The popularity of council house sales. Individual home ownership. The Open University (the apotheosis of 'do it yourself' education). The success of private health care and private education.

(v) The emergence of shop floor power in unions, the 'wild cat' strike.

(vi) The increasing independence of women with a woman being a woman in her own right and not simply ex-officio as mother of a family.

(vii) The continuing increase of car ownership, particularly the second car.

Not all these battles will go the same way, in fact corporate solutions to some may lead to compensatory individual solutions in others and vice versa. But clearly we need to create some form of leading indicators which will show how things are going. These indicators exist in economics and are greatly needed in the social field.

What are the implications for the O.R. scientist? Firstly we should become acquainted with the techniques, results and literature, of futures research. Indeed, more O.R. groups and university departments should actually be doing it. These environmental factors of the economy and technology are macro forces and we should know them, understand them and incorporate them in our modelling. Otherwise we are in danger of being reduced to the level of usefulness of bar room stewards of the *Titanic* for whom even being promoted to serving in the first class bar (which is the ambition of so many) will not significantly alter our eventual destiny.

11 Simulation Principles

'The voice is Jacob's voice but the hands are Esau's'
Book of Genesis

IT IS not the purpose of this chapter to describe the technique of simulation; this has been admirably written up elsewhere.[40, 41] The object of this chapter is to describe some of the questions which the operational research scientist should ask when approaching problems by this most powerful of all techniques. At the outset it will be wise to be clear about the difference between the Monte Carlo method and simulation. First of all, there is a good working rule that those who use the phrase 'Monte Carlo simulation' are using a glib phrase which they do not understand.

The Monte Carlo technique is a way of evaluating a deterministic problem by means of setting up a probability problem on to which it can be mapped. The probability problem is then evaluated by repeated sampling experiments and these experiments are used to evaluate the deterministic function. On the other hand an operational research simulation which uses random variables, does so because of the experimenter's ignorance of what the underlying cause-effect relationship is. Hence it is quite meaningless to use the word Monte Carlo and simulation in conjunction with each other.

For some years simulation as a method was used in a rather secretive fashion, since those who used it felt that by doing so they were confessing to a mathematical or technological ineptitude. It was thought that the proper way to solve problems was by mapping on to a mathematical language, and solving the problem within the language and the constraints of the mathematics. Hence simulation was initially developed as a way of approaching problems for which no explicit mathematical solution can be devised. However, as the method has developed it has been seen to be very powerful and to a certain extent it is now true that it is not the simulator who has to excuse himself for not using mathematics but rather the mathematician who has to excuse himself for not using simulation.

In most problems where simulation is used there are two distinct phases. The first is an understanding of the structure of the real situation in such a way that a simulation process can be deployed and the second phase is the derivation of sampling procedures by means of which the successive experiments, which lie at the heart of a simulation, can be performed.

There are in general three main reasons for using simulation. The first of these has been referred to as the case where the technical problem, be it mathematical or statistical, is too complex to be solved. The second field in which simulation is used covers those problems where the research worker needs to gain some understanding of a complex real situation and be able to manipulate it in an isomorphic form. The third type of situation is that in which the researcher is dealing with problems which do not yet exist in the real world and where one has to anticipate in advance how one should deal with them should they arise. It will be useful to take each of these briefly in turn.

The first case consists of those situations where the mathematical technique breaks down. Those who have used mathematical approaches in operational research are aware how fragile a tool is mathematics. The assumptions one has to make in order to state a problem in symbolic form may sometimes be far too great for the OR scientist to adopt them. For example, in linear programming the assumptions of linearity may often be so severe as to cause the research worker to reject the method even though it has such an appealing simplicity. In problems of queuing, any introduction of reality into the situation means that normal mathematical processes can no longer deal with the complexities involved. This is because in mathematics one is generally devising an exact solution to an approximate problem, and in order to devise these exact solutions one may sometimes be approximating far too severely. These were the original areas in which simulation first came to play a part. It would be impossible to approach the work of the British Steel Corporation (Sheffield Division) in studying the flow of production in steel-making, where there is a high degree of variability both of time and of product quality, by any formal mathematical techniques. The problem of communications in coal mines in the event of an emergency,[11] is another situation where the structure of the problem can easily be laid down, but it is one in which the mathematical processes will fail. The problems of marketing consumer products to which reference has been made in Chapter 9 is again an area in which the processes of mathematics can no longer cope. In all these situations the description of the problem is relatively simple, but even in so simplistic an area the technical competence of the mathematician is not great enough to cope. In these problems the basic task of the research worker is to understand the formal structure of the decision-making process. For example, in the problem of steel-making,[42] the task of the scientist is to map the successive stages of the flow of the steel and to impose on this the range of choice of decisions which are open to the production controller. It is understanding the relationship between what is observed to be happening and what the decision-maker may do that imposes the necessity of understanding structure. In a similar way, in the underground mining problem to which reference has been made, it was necessary to understand very precisely indeed the routine of a mine in an emergency, in such a way as to be able to see the critical points at which decisions are made and how these decisions are likely to be made in real life circumstances.

Hence, in these processes of simulation it is vital to have an understanding of the following steps.

(a) What is the basic logical connexion between the successive states of the system which is being observed?

(b) For any state of the system, what is the range of decisions open to the decision-maker?

(c) What are the transition probabilities from one state of the system to another?

(d) What effect does the decision-maker have on affecting the changes in these transition probabilities by means of the decisions which he may undertake?

It is not too much of an exaggeration to state that one of the principal virtues of a simulation approach is to force clarity of mind on the research worker in answering the above questions, whether the simulation is carried out by hand, by means of pencil and paper, or whether it is computerized. Even when the computer does all the work of sampling and decision-taking, the essential clarity will still be needed. Perhaps one of the greatest problems which the simulator faces is not so much the derivation of languages or procedures for using the simulation, but rather the difficulty he will find in answering the four questions above. Inherent in this, of course, is a sufficient understanding of the real situation in such a way as is possible to define system states in the minimum number of relevant variables. It is possible to over-simplify the definition of the state of a system in such a way that the simulation becomes trivial and arrives at solutions which are no longer appropriate in the problem. On the other hand, if the descriptive indices of system states are too great the combinatorial problem involved in the transitional probabilities becomes so large as to defeat the experimenter. This conflict between complexity and reality lies at the core of many of the difficulties of using the simulation approach. We should, however, always remember Ackoff's aphorism that the greater the understanding we have of a system, the fewer variables we shall need to describe it.[7]

The second reason for using a simulation approach is to gain an understanding of a complex situation. In this, one is not so much seeking to solve a specific problem, but rather to understand how the system is working. In this area one is generally thinking rather more freely or admitting hypotheses based on far less evidence than in the preceding example where we depend on an accurate description of causes and effects. The reason for trying to gain an understanding of the system is precisely because we do not have this comprehension of the relationship between patterns of causes and patterns of effects. Hence this particular approach to simulation may well precede that of the first kind to which reference has been made. In these approaches one is formulating hypotheses in the absence of data and perhaps even in the absence of observations. Typical in this are the hypotheses one may make about marketing behaviour and the reaction of consumers to advertising price, promotions, distribution and so on. The basic model (p. 113) was an example of an approach where in the absence of relevant data one formulated a tentative hypothesis of what ought to be going on, if life has any reason associated with it. In these situations one forms an imitation of the real world and then manipulates it to see whether it reacts like reality. For example we may take an analogy of simulating a bicycle in such a way that if we sit on the simulator and pedal and move the handlebars, our feel for the balance and the response of the system makes us think that we are on an actual bicycle. In the same way, therefore, in this form of simulation we depend critically on having the model manipulated by those who take the decisions in the real world, in order for us to have some confidence that what we have built into the simulator replicates the processes of the real world. This is essentially the black box approach in which one inserts the black box certain mechanisms and then turns the knobs on the outside to see whether the same sort of thing happens as in life.

There are two ways of looking at and estimating the mechanisms which should go inside the black box. These correspond with the descriptive and explanatory approaches of Ackoff and Rivett.[9] For example, we may predicate as a hypothesis a relation between certain variables in the complex situation of reality, and insert this relationship as an attempt at an explanatory model. The second way of inserting relationships within the black box is to carry out controlled statistical experiments, as a result of which we are able to establish the relationship between some of the variables out of the multiplicity of factors which may be operating. In general it is very difficult to do this, as it is almost impossible to hold the level of the remaining variables constant, while we experiment with the relationship between two of them.

The art in this form of simulation is, by some intuitive means, to create a model within which a simulation can take place which responds to the experienced man as the real world responds. This may take some time, and will ceratinly involve the scientist in spending time and trouble in gaining insight into the likely relationships which exist in the real situation. Once this time has been invested, however, it then becomes possible to gain a considerable dividend from this approach, which is to learn and gain experience rapidly in a wide range of conditions, outside the bounds of the original model. This form of simulation, therefore, gives one the opportunity of learning rapidly in conditions in which it is possible to survive catastrophes. It has, as a result, two advantages. First of all, it enables one to learn rapidly and secondly it enables one to survive mistakes. In this form of simulation one has to start, as far as possible, with conditions which represent the real situation and then move beyond them by means of changing the variables or even, to a certain extent, changing the structure of the cause-effect relationships.

The third area in which simulation methods are used is that in which we are dealing with situations which have not yet occurred and for which we hope to be prepared. War-gaming is essentially one such situation. In war games[43] one is not only making assumptions about the structural relationships of the variables which are involved and the probabilities of transition from one state of the system to another, but one is also able to make assumptions and inject into the analysis such questions as, 'If we had a weapons system with these characteristics what effect would it have on certain kinds of battle?' The parallels of this in the problems of research and development are obvious. We can use the simulation approach in industrial terms to replicate a real situation, and then to see how it would change and what the effect would be on the development of new technologies, new processes, new materials or new machines. This can then give some insight into how much it is worth spending on particular types of research and development, in order that the pay-off from the investment should be worthwhile. This form of simulation is nowhere near as developed as the others and often suffers from the fact that the time period over which the simulation takes place is greater than the comparable time period of real life. In war-gaming, for example, the time it takes to work through even simple battles, by means of a simulation process, may be far longer than the time the actual battle would take to be fought. Were there the opportunities of gaining experience from real battles, this form of simulation would not take place since the learning process of reality would outsrip the learning process of the simulation. It is, however, because the reality does not yet exist that this form of simulation process becomes important.

It cannot be emphasized too strongly that in all of the above three approaches it is necessary, not only thoroughly to understand the structural relationships which one has assumed in the real situation, but also to state these explicitly so that other experimenters know the assumptions under which one has proceeded. The author knows of no simulation process in which this time period for gaining understanding has not greatly exceeded the time over which the simulation is actually used in an experimental fashion. It is as though we are producing living beings in which the gestation period greatly exceeds the period of life in the world.

An important phase in simulation is the opportunity of computerizing the whole process. In general it is the case that the intial stages of gaining understanding, will involve manual operations in preliminary simulation runs. Very rapidly, however, the whole process has to be computerized and one has to face two problems. The first of these is the derivation of a language within which the computerization and simulation can take place. There are many languages available, some of them specialized to particular forms of problem and others of a more general and perhaps sometimes less useful type. There is a first-class description of the problem of language derivation and language use in a paper by Tocher.[42] The second problem is the derivation of populations from which the samples shall be taken and which are going to give the values used in each simulation run. This is a technical problem in the field of statistics and probability and may sometimes appear to be more important than the stsructure of the simulation itself. Many articles and papers written on simulation reduce very rapidly to the problem of random number generation. Obviously this is important. When one is computerizing the process, one has to be certain that the samples one is taking to generate the successive simulation runs are truly 'random', however random may be defined. If it is not so then there is the danger that the results of the experiment may be biased and misleading. But there is more in simulation than random number generation, and it is important for the scientist who uses this technology to be quite clear of the other matters which have been outlined above, as well as this particular problem of random number generation which often seems to occupy too much space in the simulation literature.

As can be seen, one of the abiding difficulties of simulation is that it is generally undertaken in those circumstances in which we are trying to speed up the real world. Furthermore it is used in situations where it may well not be possible to take the implementations of the solution piecemeal, and hence in applying the solution one may well be faced precisely with the trial and catastrophe situation that one has tried to avoid by developing a simulation approach. It is necessary therefore to try to clarify some of the ways in which a simulation can be tested before its conclusions are applied in practice. Probably the best tests of validation are those given by Hermann.[44] These five kinds of validation are:

(1) 'Internal Validity', that is, does the simulation have a low variance of outputs when replicated with all the external inputs held constant? If there is a high variance in the results due to the internal processes, then one may well question whether the black box relations which have been assumed adequately reflect the real world.

(2) Does the model react reasonably when manipulated either by the experimenter or, better, by the on-line, real life decision-maker?

(3) Do the relationship between the variables within the simulation correspond to those of real life? For example, is the simulation as sensitive in its reaction to changes in the parameters as the real world appears to be? To a certain extent as can be seen, this is a quantification of (2) above.

(4) To what extent does the simulation enable one to predict observable events or event patterns? For example, if we apply the simulation to points in history do we then see happening with the simulation the same kind of pattern of events as happened in the real world?

(5) Do the relationships between pairs of observations within the simulation correspond to the same relationships between these pairs as observed in the real world? This is characterized by Hermann as 'Hypothesis Validity' (see also a paper by Sisson[41]).

At its heart it is fair to say that the application of simulation models involves an act of faith. In saying this, however, we have to realize that the application of most operational research models involves acts of faith. Even in the apparent clarity of the deterministic processes of linear programming one will have made assumptions which mean that the solution will have to be applied as an act of faith. Within the simulation process, the points at which faith is necessary are quite clear, but perhaps the greatest virtue of simulation to the model builder is that it is the bridge which most closely links him with the mainstream of classical science. Within the terms of a simulation it is possible to experiment in a way that one is unable to achieve in any other approach in decision-making. It is for this reason, if for no other, that the model builder must always first ask the question, 'Is it possible that the problem I am studying can be understood, clarified or even solved by adopting a simulation approach?' It is perhaps not too much of an exaggeration to say that one does not decide whether to contract *in* to simulation, but whether one should contract out of it.

12 Organizational Objectives

'Can two walk together except they be agreed?'

Amos

AS WAS suggested in the earlier chapters, although to be logical it is necessary to comprehend the objectives of an organization before a model is built, it is nearly always the case that the objectives only become clear during the course of the construction of the model. We have also made a distinction between objectives, goals and performance criteria and we shall return to this distinction at a later stage in this particular chapter.

The definition of organizational objective which we have used in this book is a long term state towards which the organization is hopefully proceeding. This long term state may be unattainable and may be recognised as being unattainable but nevertheless is still worthy of attempt. Secondly, the progress towards the objectives is measured in terms of goals which are functions of time but the objectives themselves do not have any time of achievement set against them; if they do then they become goals rather than objectives. Finally, the purpose of the objective is to provide, at the highest level of an organization, a statement against which all decisions in the organization can be tested and from which all decision-making criteria should stem. Hence, the objectives are in essence a statement of the character of an organization.

Having stated this it is not inappropriate to quote Stevenson.[59]

'A strange picture we make on our way to our dreams, ceaselessly marching, grudging ourselves the time for rest: (indefatigable, adventurous pioneers). It is true that we shall never reach the goal—it is even more probable that there is no such place. Soon, soon, it seems to you, you must come forth on some conspicuous hilltop, and but a little way farther, against the setting sun, descry the spire of El Dorado. Little do ye know your own blessedness, for to travel hopefully is a better thing than to arrive, and the true success is to labour.'

It is specifically in this spirit that we have used the term 'objective' in this book. In this chapter we shall consider the matter of organizational objectives from three aspects. In the first we shall survey organizational objectives as they appear at the time of writing this book, so that we can estimate the extent to which business organizations in particular, and other organizations generally, have formal statements of objectives and goals. We shall then survey some theoretical approaches to the problem of considering weighting coefficients that can be assigned to various objectives which an organization may have. In the final section of this chapter we shall suggest the criteria that all objectives should satisfy in order to be useful.

Organizational objectives as they exist

During 1970, the author carried out a survey of over 300 organizations in the United Kingdom. The main bulk of these were industrial, including both the private and the nationalized sectors. In addition approaches were made to a number of non-industrial systems such as Government departments, including Defence, Universities and other social institutions such as hospitals. These organizations were asked the extent to which there was any explicit statement of the organizational objectives and/or goals and the extent to which this statement was comprehended by management at different levels. These questions were addressed to operational research and management scientists in the organizations, who were also asked whether they had any part in setting these goals or objectives and the extent to which they thought they were adequate and realistic. A final question was whether they would like the opportunity of up-dating organizational objectives and whether they would feel competent to do so if requested.

Replies were received from 120 organizations. Of these, about 50 were simple statements that such problems as objectives, goals and criteria had either not been studied in the organization or the operational research leader concerned had no knowledge of, or interest in, them. There was left therefore a residuum of some 70 replies. These were quite extensive and in the main were lengthy and highly confidential. It was obvious that the enquiries had touched a significant willingness to respond.

As a crude classification one could divide those who replied into two groups: the private sector of the economy, and those in the other sector which would include nationalized industries, government departments, universities, research associations, etc.

A large number of research groups did not know of any explicit statement by their organizations of their objectives and goals. This was rather depressing. It is curious to understand how an OR group can advise an organization of what courses of action it should adopt, if the criteria by which courses of action are being judged are not known. Amongst the replies, however, there were some interesting and revealing statements. (It will be appreicated that most of these have to be treated in confidence.)

We may first of all quote those statements of objective which, while apparently useful, on a deeper study reveal themselves as being not very helpful. For example, the British Steel Corporation is on record with the following statement, 'The corporation regards its basic objective as being the achievement of the maximum long term return on its capital investment consistent with (a) strengthening its marketing and technological position in the world steel industry, (b) providing British industry with products that are competitive in price, quality and service and (c) ensuring the efficient and socially responsible utilisation of human resources'. Such a statement, without any means given for quantifying the various objectives, nor any statement of the trade-off between degrees of attainment of different objectives, does not aid decisions in the allocation of resources.

In the nationalization act for the Gas Industry it is stated that one duty of the Industry is 'to meet the demand for their products and services in the most efficient way and to conduct their finances so that over a period they at least break even, after making a contribution to reserves.' This is another example of lack of quantification and of definition of terms. Another industry, which must be nameless, has as its stated objective 'to provide the most efficient service possible at lowest cost consistent with sound financial policies'. 'This again is not geared to enable purposeful decision-making to be undertaken. Unfortunately, amongst all these, some of the management consulting groups do not emerge as models of clarity. One group, for example, is proud that their objectives have remained unchanged for the last thirty years (it is pleasant to know that there are some fixed points in a changing world) and also quotes themselves as having the objective 'to be the leading management consulting group in the world'. This is meaningless unless one defines what is meant by leadership and what one means by management consulting, i.e. what is their market? As a final example of these unhelpful general statements, one well-known private company includes amongst its objectives 'to maintain an aggressive posture in the market'. This is an emotional statement.

The reaction of operational research workers to their own organizational objectives, where they existed, and the comments they made on them were revealing. One internationally known research worker-stated 'without claiming to have an exhaustive list of our specific objectives and goals, I do know that our goal is to increase productivity by $"x"$ per cent in three years, where $"x"$ has been specified, but I have forgotten the value'. Another head of an OR group: 'the only information I gather about our Company's objectives is what I read in its image advertising'.

It was possible, however, to draw certain general conclusions regarding the nature of organizational objectives, where they exist. It was interesting to analyse them according to the extent of quantitative statements within the set of objectives. In general it appeared that the nationalized industries had led down for them, either by Act of Parliament or by Ministerial directive, sets of objectives and goals which were dominantly quantitative. This was surprising. One imagines that the goals of the nationalized industries would have incorporated within them some social statement and function. Certainly, apart from general statements regarding service to customers (which are common to all companies, private or nationalized), it was not possible to distinguish in any of the statements any form of social consciousness. Those who have worked in the nationalized industries know that their decision-making is socially very responsible. There are always financial pressures upon them, as is only right, but they operate by choice within a social climate. Consequently one was led to question whether the objectives of these nationalized industries, as laid down solely in terms of profit and cost, were real objectives or whether they had a public relations flavour.

Other organizations, notably in the private sector, did incorporate in their objectives certain statements of service to the community. The published objectives of the International Publishing Corporation, for example, run to two pages in length, are socially conscious in terms and have many statements about the relationship of IPC with its suppliers, its customers, its workers and with the community generally. Another company—one of Britain's most exclusively cost-conscious and profit-dominated companies—has a set of objectives which are almost purely social in character. They refer to the company forming a bond of service and mutual regard with its suppliers, workers, the local community, its customers and the national government and so on. The distinction between the written objectives of this company and the way in which it appears to operate is surprising, to say the least. Again, one is forced to ask the question of the extent to which formalized statements of objectives of this nature are meant as a basis for decision-making or as a public relations exercise.

There were a number of points of specific note. First of all, within the replies from the private enterprise companies it was interesting to note that only two of the 30 organizations in this group had any mention of the shareholders. It must be confessed that although standard management all refer to textbooks the dominance of the shareholders' interests in decision-making it is rare, if ever, that one is present at any executive discussion in a company in which the shareholders are specifically mentioned. They are, of course, implicitly covered in the three main areas and topics which were common to most of the replies which were received. These three basic objectives of organizations emerged as:

(a) *Survival*. Nearly all organizations have implicit within their statement of goals and objectives, the need for the organization to survive. Sometimes within the private sector survival of the organization is taken as being synonymous with survival of the senior management, particularly if a take-over battle is in prospect. However, it is natural that survival should underpin decision-making, as is apparent to anyone who has taken part in large-scale investment decisions in a probabilistic climate. Some socially conscious organizations, such as a Cancer Research Fund, may actually work for their disappearance but these are rare exceptions.

(b) *Growth*. Almost without exception, every organization wanted to grow, however one defines growth. It is curious how widespread is the desire for growth. One company had an explicit statement that it wished to have a growth of net earnings per share. Another investment group (which shortly after this research ran into embarrassing difficulties) had as its objective 'to be the largest financial institution in the world'. Desires for growth, if not to so great extent, underpinned almost every statement of organizational objectives. This is not only the case within the private sector. (Even such unwordly institutions as universities wish to grow. One has yet to meet a Vice-Chancellor who does not wish his university to increase in size.) Generally, growth seems to be inbuilt into our socio-economic systems as some form of manifest destiny. Even those organizations which are unlikely to grow are anxious to have a minimum rate of decline. One can ask why it is, for example, that some nationalized industries, which require their workers to operate in unpleasant or dangerous conditions, will fight desperately against closure, even though alternative sources of supply of the industry's product may be available and it may well be the social gain of the whole community that such industries should decline. These particular industries are not run by antisocial, inhuman monsters. They are run by humane, socially conscious management of a high degree of purposefulness, and yet the inbuilt desire to grow, or at least to arrest decline, is manifest in every decision.

(c) *Maximization of well-being.* This is different from maximization of profitability, and indeed only one organization out of those who replied had maximization of profitability as an objective. It seems well understood that profitability is not an end but a means to an end. Most managers, particularly in the higher echelon, wish to enjoy what they are doing. Profitability at a level which enables them to deal with the shareholders' needs, to ensure the survival of the organization, means that from then on management can start to enjoy themselves. Goodeve's use of the word 'eudemeny' to describe this state of well-being is very apt.[45]

We see, therefore, that the statement of organizational objectives is by no means simple (in every case except one there was more than one objective) and the means of establishing trade-offs between degrees of attainment of different objectives is going to be important in the model-building process.

Having dealt at some length with the first question, the replies to the other questins are more straightforward. Almost without exception no operational research group has been concerned in the setting of organizational objectives. In some cases they have made comments on the process of setting organizational objectives but most groups have been kept separate from this process.

The adequacy and realism of the statements of objectives was supported by approximately half of the heads of OR groups who expressed an opinion. Many were uneasy about their objectives and many pointed to inbuilt contradictions within them. In addition, wherever unease was expressed it was expressed in terms of concern at the lack of quantification of the objectives. In most of these cases whenever attempts have been made to use statements of organizational objectives, it has been found impossible to use them as an aid to decision-making because of the lack of a quantitative support structure.

Most respondents wanted the opportunity of updating objectives and felt that they were competent to do so. On the other hand there were some rather depressing pockets of apathy. One head of OR, for example, stated that he felt 'it would be impertinent for him as a mere operational research scientist to comment on his organization's objectives'.

Theoretical treatment of organizational objectives

We are, of course, in a pragmatic sense, not concerned with organizational objectives but with the consequences of organizational policies. To understand objectives is *a* means to the end, but is not the only means. We first of all consider the treatment of objectives and of degrees of attainment of them and then proceed to an alternative method which retains the integrity of a policy without breaking it down into separate (objective related) parts.

There have been a number of treatments of organizational objectives with a view to dealing with the following problems. Suppose we have a set of objectives 0_1, 0_2, etc. and we have to rank these objectives on a common scale of measurement. One way of achieving this is to make a direct appeal to utility theory. In this we shall rank the objectives in ascending order of desirability and then, as in Chapter 8, we shall consider a lottery in which the most desirable objective is the winning prize and the least desirable objective is the losing prize. Then, for any objective between these two extremes, we shall form an indifference lottery by stating the percentage of winning tickets in a lottery with winning and losing prizes as stated, against which we would be indifferent to taking part in this lottery and receiving any other objectives for certain.

Suppose our five objectives can be ranked in the following order of merit 0_1 (least desirable); 0_2; 0_3; 0_4; 0_5 (most desirable). In this way one can assign a utility index to any course of action but this is severely constrained by two basic assumptions.

First of all we make the assumption that it is possible to rank the objectives in an order of merit, and also to derive the probability with which any course of action will achieve any one of the objectives. The second objection to this particular formulation is that the objectives themselves must be mutually exclusive and hence one can only achieve an objective either completely or miss it absolutely. This, of course, does impose a grave impediment on the realism of this formulation. In real life it is not often the case that either we completely gain an objective or completely fail to achieve it. For example, if the objective is a 20 per cent share of market, it would be unrealistic to say that an 18 per cent share of market is of zero value while a 23 per cent share of market is of unitary value. This, together with the demand of mutual exclusivity on the achievement of the objectives, renders this particular approach of no great practical use. However, the method is useful in formulating a basic understanding of the relative importance of different objectives which an organization may have.

In order to avoid the restrictive condition of mutual exclusivity, Ackoff[46] has proposed a method as follows.

Rank the objectives in order of value,

$$0_1 \text{ (most preferred)}, 0_2, 0_3, \ldots 0_n \text{ (least preferred)}$$

Assign value 1·0 to 0_1, and take a trial set V_2, V_3, ..., V_n for the others.

Compare 0_1 with all the others. If 0_1 is preferred to all the others, is

$$1 \cdot 0 > V_2 + V_3 + \ldots + V_n?$$

If not, adjust the $V_i(i = 1)$ such that $1 \cdot 0 > V_2 + \ldots + V_n$

If 0_1 is not preferred to the others, adjust the V_i if necessary, so that

$$1 < V_2 + V_3 + \ldots + V_n.$$

Now omit 0_n and carry on with this procedure so as to derive a feasible set of V_i that satisfy all tests of the form, that if one group of objectives is preferred to another group, then the sum of its V's is greater than that of the other group.

The objection to this procedure is largely the same as the objection to the earlier procedure, except that we have now removed the problem of mutual exclusiveness of the objective. For example, we still have to use the concept that an objective is either completely obtained or completely non-obtained and that there is not point in between these two extremes. These two approaches, however, do enable one to deal in part with the problem of many objectives.

One of the most useful approaches to this problem is one suggested by Gupta[47] who has formulated a method of dealing with any degree of attainment of an objective which can be assessed against any number of alternative courses of action. The constraint in the Gupta method as it is presently formulated, is that only two objectives can be dealt with. The summary of his approach is to assign to two courses of action A and B, with a certain outcome for each, the results π^A and π^B. There are n relevant criteria (qualitative) for each; hence we have to compare the two sets of results π^A_i and π^B_i $(i = 1, \ldots, n)$.

The method assumes: (i) the decision-maker can state whether or not he prefers each π^A_i to each π^B_i; (ii) there exists a real valued scalar function $u(\pi)$ with continuous first derivatives, whose domain is a se Ω of alternatives which produces a unique ordering over all elements of Ω. The function $u(\pi)$ is the decision-maker's utility.

The method approximates to
$$u(\pi^A) - u(\pi^B) \text{ by } (\pi^A - \pi^B)^1(\text{grad } u)\pi = \pi^*$$

where π^* lies between π^A and π^B. Since the vector $(\pi^A - \pi^B)^1$ is known, knowledge of the gradient of u is sufficient to determine whether or not $u(\pi^A) > u(\pi^B)$. It is necessary however for π^A and π^B to be 'close together'. The method makes an appeal to the decision-maker's marginal substitution rate between pairs of the objectives and formulates a linear programming model to create bounds on the elements of the gradient of u such that the sign of $u(\pi^A) - u(\pi^B)$ will remain unchanged for all feasible grad u.

As can be seen, therefore, the basic approaches depend on an appeal either to some form of utility theory approach with its all or nothing assumption or, alternatively, they can only handle at most two competing objectives. Clearly there is scope for more research in this area but, equally clearly, such research should be firmly entrenched in the real objective formulation of organizations.

An alternative approach

The methods so far outlines are all reductionist. That is, they break down the results of a policy into the separate parts according to the separate goals and objectives and firstly evaluate the degrees of attainment of each of the goals. The second stage is to bring these parts together to create some index or single measure of the overall attractiveness of the policy.

An alternative method[48, 49, 50] retains the integrity of the policy specifically by *not* breaking it down into parts but by dealing with it as a whole. The method utilises both the techniques of multi-dimensional scaling (Kruskal[51, 52]) and their application to archaeological problems as developed by Kendall.[53, 54, 55] What the method takes as input is a consideration of all possible pairs of policies and a listing of those particular pairs which the decision maker feels are roughly equally attractive. The technique then produces maps of these policies in which roughly equally attractive policies are placed near each other (note that such policies can be quite *different* in nature) and these preference maps tend to throw to polar extremities the sub-sets of most preferred and least preferred policies. The position of a policy along the principal axis of the map can be taken as a quantitative measure of its attractiveness and it appears to have a close relation with utility while making much less severe axiomatic demands.

Consider the following example which is taken from Rivett.[48] In this, alternative ways (policies) are taken, of allocating a fixed total expenditure between different possible expenditures (objectives):

(a) Old people's housing.
(b) Pre-natal-care centres.
(c) Post-natal-care centres.
(d) Coronary units.

For each of these objectives the author formulated a plausible relation between expenditure on that particular objective (cause) and the result in terms of old people's bungalows built, or reduction in still born or defective infants, etc. (effect). Twenty-four different ways were taken of allocating this same total expenditure between the four objectives. Each of the 276 pairs of policies were examined and a note was kept of all those pairs, (links), the members of which appeared roughly equally attractive (or repulsive) to the author. Preference maps were constructed by allotting a distance of 1 between two policies which were linked, a distance 2 between two policies which while not immediately linked are nevertheless each linked to a third policy, and a distance n (> 2) for all the remaining pairs. Kendall has shown[53, 54] that such a simple metric can produce topologically accurate maps. In this case the (two dimensional maps, each starting from a different random configuration of points, all led, by iteration, to a very similar final layout and a typical map is shown in Figure 44. (In this map, lines join pairs of policies which had indifference links allocated by the author's assessment.)

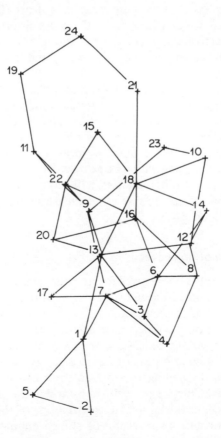

Figure 44. Two-dimensional policy map

It was clear to the author that he greatly preferred the triad 19, 21, 24, to the triad 1, 2, 5 and hence the inferrence was that the principal axis (drawn here up the page) is the axis of preference and the polar groups represent most and least preferred policies.

It would be silly to use such a process for selecting a single 'best' policy, but it appears a useful way of deriving a shortlist.

Further developments of the method have taken the case where every policy has a single value and where pre-assigned probability laws are used to determine whether or not a pair of policies are linked. Results indicate that the mapping process puts the points corresponding to the policies in relative positions along the principal axis of the configuration which are highly correlated with the prior values. A method has also been derived (Rivett[56]) which gives a good estimate of the probability law used to assign links.

These methods have been applied to the above example of social expenditure to provide of the internal mental processes (and mental confusion) of the author.[57]

For such methods to be useful there must be at least 10 alternative policies and each policy must have at least two others which are perceived as being roughly equally attractive. An important relaxation of a troublesome axiom in utility theory is that transitivity is not necessary, that is $A \sim B$ and $B \sim C$ does not imply $A \sim C$.

The most important stumbling block in utility is its failure to deal with group decision making. However, it does appear that preference mapping may offer a way of dealing with groups of people. As a method it has the advantage of being less demanding axiomatically than Utility Theory while suffering the disadvantage of requiring a minimum number of alternative policies. The combinatorial problem arising with a large number of policies is not as serious as may appear. Although thirty policies will have 435 pairs, recent research into robustness of maps seems to show that the actual number of comparisons to be made may be much less.

An ideal formulation of objectives

In formulating basic sets of objectives for an organization one point should be made quite clear. It is insufficient to formulate objectives without any consideration of the effect of these objectives on the performance and functioning of the organization. For example, once a statement of objectives has been formulated it is necessary to consider a series of alternative goals which the organization should achieve on each of a number of successive years, as part of a progress towards these objectives. When these goals have been stated it is then necessary to formulate the procedures by which the goals are going to be achieved. These procedures will involve calculations of the rate of generation of resources, in particular the provision of skilled manpower, adequate cash flow, adequate managerial competence to monitor cash flow and capital investment, the availability of raw material and the development of market potential.

Clearly this process now becomes circular. Having stated a tentative set of objectives, this is translated into organizational goals and the goals themselves are then examined by feasibility studies which show the implication of the achievement of these goals in terms of the total work and performance of the organization. If this feasibility study shows that the goals are unlikely to be achieved because of particular bottle-necks in, for example, either supply of raw material or demand for products, then it is necessary to restate the goal. It must be emphasized that, in general, the objectives remain above this cyclic battle of goals and feasibility study. The reason for this is that the statement of the objectives is a statement of what sort of organization is required. It is sometimes the case that organizational objectives are changed but this is a change of the character and nature of an organization, rather than a change of temporal goals. Consequently, although goals may be updated and changed quite frequently, the organizational objectives will tend to be much more constant in nature, since they will tend to reflect the aspirations and motivations of the sum total of personnel involved.

What then, can we say should be covered in any statement of organizational objectives, bearing in mind that these objectives will describe the character and nature of the organization?

Firstly the organization should state, in some measured form, the importance it places on survival. This will involve a consideration of the relationships between risk and expectation of return. The extent to which survival means survival of the organization as it now stands should be made clear. Alternatively does it mean the survival of the present management and in particular the present board of directors? Does it mean survival in terms of offering employment at a given level to a certain number of work people, or does it mean paramountly the survival of the shareholders' equity?

Secondly the objectives should have some statement of the view that is taken of growth. As has been seen, growth is almost an imperative of organizations and we need to consider why this should be so. Often it is not clear why an organization should want to expand. One reason might be that in order to attract lively dynamic staff to an organization, it is necessary for them to feel that this is a growing concern. Beyond that, however, the normal requirements of growth need justification and should not be taken as being self-evident. If the organization requires growth as part of its statement of objectives, then these objectives should include ways of measuring growth. Is this measured in terms of sales? If so, how are these sales to be measured—by volume or by cash input? Is growth to be measured by share of market? To what extent does increasing the number of personnel in the organization reflect desire for growth? Is the company concerned with growth in terms of the geographical area in which it operates, either in production or marketing? Does growth mean growth in earnings per share for the shareholder, in profits (in which case we have to take out the effect of inflation) or in profitability (however that most elusive of concepts is defined)? What is the relative importance of these and what trade-offs exist?

Thirdly, we need some formulation of what the organization defines as the well-being which it wishes to maximize. This will involve some consideration of the trade-off between profitability and other non-financial and social objectives. It will be a difficult subject for the organization to address itself to, but it is necessary to have some formal statement of the extent to which social purposes can intrude on the normal profit-making organization of business.

Finally, there will be statements in the objectives which cover the nature of the organization and its responsibilities to the community in which it is placed. To what extent is the organization concerned with its environment? What responsibility does it take for this? Is it going to be an innovative organization or is it going to be imitative? If innovative, how is innovation to be measured? To what extent does the organization look on itself as having responsibilities to its employees; to what extent is it concerned with employee morale; and, if this is important, how is morale measured? What is the form of the relationship the organization has with its suppliers and customers? If it requires high standards of customers satisfaction, how is such satisfaction to be measured? To what extent is the organization willing to subordinate its own selfish purposes in terms of the national good? (Selfish is not used in a pejorative sense.) Does it wish, for example, to develop export business as a means of assisting the economy of the country, or will export business have to be subservient to the normal profit motive?

We suggest that this minimal list is necessary in any statement of organizational objectives. Whenever an objective has been suggested in the above list we have also made the request that the form of measurement should also be stated. It cannot be too strongly emphasized that any statement of objectives which does not have attached to it the method of measurement, is likely to be a mere statement of intent and will be useless in enabling those who are concerned with goal formulation to suggest temporal goals for the organization.

The responsibility of the researcher

To what extent should the operational researcher be concerned with this process? We may reflect in passing that in most operational research studies, either objectives are taken by default or alternatively when, they are laid down, the operational researcher will propose models which are generally bad at showing the extent to which objectives are likely to be obtained. One reason for this is that there may be a number of statements of objectives and no means are proposed by their organization either of measuring their attainment or of ranking their importance. This means that the operational researcher will often content himself with formulating models which deal solely with one of these objectives. If this is what he does, then although he may have taken some of the indecision out of the management problem, he has not made a really serious contribution to removing the doubt and uncertainty which cloud so much decision-making.

The conclusion to which one is drawn is that the operational researcher should feel competent to discuss the organizational objectives, although he may well be somewhat loath to suggest changes in them since this involves changing the character of the organization. He should certainly, however, feel competent to suggest those objectives which have not yet been stated, and he must always be prepared to comment on and to propose means of measuring degrees of attainment of objectives. It is no longer sufficient for the operational researcher to accept a statement of objectives and goals as given and then merely to provide some form of model which shows how these goals and objectives might best be obtained. He must, if he is to serve the organization correctly, be intimately concerned with the processes of objective formulation and goal statement. Anything less than this is a severe form of sub-optimization which means that the researcher is not serving the organization to the best of his ability.

13 Summary

'Of the things we have spoken, this is the sum'
Epistle to the Hebrews

Difficulties in the operational research approach

Certain assumptions are made in all model-building, which need to be explicitly stated since when they are stated we are likely to ponder the extent to which our model building is justified.

We make four assumptions in the model-building process. The first is that during the progress of a piece of research the organization will not change. To be facetious, we assume that we can stop the world, get off and build a model. Those who have been concerned with the modelling approach will know that this is not the case. It is not unusual for a research team to discover, at the end of its investigation, that the organization has adopted the policy which it was recommending before it has even read the report. This is not necessarily wrong, since the research itself has probably acted as a catalyst. If there has been proper communication between the research team and the organization, and if there is an adequate degree of faith in the organization about the competence of the research team, then it may well be that implementation will take place before completion of the study. On the other hand, however, there are more serious situations. In research studies which take a long time it is difficult constantly to up-date the study in the light of fresh information, fresh evidence and fresh knowledge of the changing environment. Additionally, it will be discovered that senior personnel in an organization may change during the progress of a study, and hence the sets of objectives which are going to be dealt with, and the ranking of these objectives, is going to be affected. This latter is not so important as the former. A method of dealing with objectives which enables them to be ranked and to be subsumed under one single parameter, will not have much difficulty in dealing with the situation which arises when this ranking changes. On the other hand, as has been stated in the chapter on model building and objective functions, the sets of objectives towards which the organization is working, will determine the form of the model which is built, since certain models are much better at dealing with certain kinds of objectives, than others. If during the progress of the study the objectives of the organization are changed significantly, then the research team will discover that they have reported on a non-problem. This is not unusual. The extent to which our model building may be invalid, because the speed at which the research can be carried out is too slow compared with the rate of change in the organization, may well be questionable.

The second assumption which one makes is akin to the first. We demand of the organizations we serve that they should indicate to us unique points of decision at which it is possible to construct a model. One observes that when large decisions are reached the room for manoeuvre in these decisions may have been pre-empted by a number of smaller decisions which have already been taken. The unique large decision, while having an attraction and glambour associated with it, is not as frequent nor as important as the series of small decisions which affects the ambience of an organization. There is a need to develop ways of modelling which can be used and developed within a continuum of decisions. This is quite a different approach from that of the single unique decision and it is particularly interesting that Ackoff[7] has developed this concept within the terms of corporate planning.

This leads to the third assumption. We need to discover the extent to which optimality is simply a chimera and optimization is irrelevant. As shown in Chapter 12, one of the basic objectives of an organization is simply to survive. A consequence of this is that given survival there is not a compelling need to optimize. Most operational research models are committed to finding extreme values of functions; that is, they are optimizing models. Mathematical programming, for example, will tell us nothing at all about the second best solution. It is rare indeed that a model builder using linear programming will deliberately calculate the worst possible answer and compare it with the best possible, in order to see the extent to which it is necessary to be concerned with the problem anyway. We must question the extent to which our model-building processes and the mathematics of model solution, by giving us a unique best answer, are failing to provide us with a whole set of solutions which achieve certain minimum characteristics and hence are acceptable to the organization. This is the approach of satisfycing.[10]

The fourth assumption which one makes on the requirements in model building, is perhaps the most difficult to discuss. We have to make the assumption that the executive on whose behalf the study is being carried out has a set of objectives which are mutually consistent with one another and which remain constant over time. This is manifestly and universally untrue. We have seen above, the way in which a group of people with perfectly consistent logic may break the transitivity assumption of utility theory. It is almost inevitably the case that each one of us, if our objectives in life were analysed in any constructive logically connected fashion, would show that we have these inconsistencies. Does this now mean that the executive must change, and be consistent? Or does it mean that our model-building approach must recognize this inconsistency? If so, in what way should the approach be adapted to recognize inconsistency, and can the processes of science be used if we have this basic inconsistency? And if the processes of science cannot be used, why build models?

The constancy of objectives is another untenable characteristic of executives and individuals. Those who observe a committee at work will notice that their powers of discrimination will change through the committee meeting. The perceptive chairman will put the items on which he places most value, at the end of a long agenda, because he will know that they then will have the most chance of being accepted. Every director will be known by his staff according to the days and periods on which it is wise and prudent to take matters to him for acceptance and those days on which it is wise and prudent to avoid him completely. We can ask the question, therefore, of the extent to which objectives will change. It is not jusst the case that individuals have whims and peccadillos which we recognize and learn to love. Serious matters in large organizations can sometimes be taken one way, at a particular moment in time, because of a wind of emotion sweeping the organization, whereas a year or even a month later a different decision might be taken simply because the emotional climate has changed. This emotional climate will have nothing to do with costs and revenues and nothing to do with value judgements as used in the utility theory form. But it will have everything to do with people and organizations.

One hopes that the above analysis is not too depressing. We have to remember, however, that if we are to serve our subject properly we must have a proper appreciation of its faults and weaknesses. The strong advocate for any topic is the man who can argue convincingly the opposing case. One only appreciates the strength of a discipline by understanding its weaknesses.

Variety of models

In this chapter we shall attempt to draw together some of the major points made earlier in this book; and, at the same time, we shall try to put them within the context of the total task of the operational researcher.

It is a truth sometimes forgotten, that the problems which we solve do not exist in themselves in any concrete form. The problems of management exist only in the minds of managers and in the minds of their advisers. There is, therefore, a completely subjective personal basis to our science. It is not the case that a company has an inventory problem, in the sense that if you visit it you can see it there in concrete form. The inventory problem which the company has exists in our own minds as expressing an out of balance in the way in which various probabilistics of supply and demands have been uncoupled. A company does not have a transportation problem existing for certain; all we can say is that it exists in our minds. This is not merely an interesting philosophical point, but it pinpoints the conclusion that there can be no such thing as an optimal model for any management situation. Even within our own minds as we approach a practical problem we will be unsure how to show which form of model is likely to be optimal. As has been seen, models which describe the situation more accurately may not be appropriate models for deriving solutions for management action. Since the problems as seen in each of our minds will be different, and mutual comparison will be impossible, it follows that we have a significant, even dangerous freedom in the way in which we select the models which will represent decision-making situations.

The danger which has been referred to is that one of the consequences of such freedom (which would be the possibility of a variety of experimental approaches to decision-making by means of various models) is denied us because in practical circumstances it is impossible to compare differing modelling approaches. This is denied us not only for temporal considerations, namely that once we have completed one approach circumstances will have changed and it will be impossible to have a comparative approach, but also because if we carry out two approaches different in nature but parallel to and simultaneously with each other, we shall then find that we are acting on the situation in a way different from that if we were adopting only one of these approaches. Finally, of course, the costs of an operational research study, in terms of their effect on people and the demands we make on their time, will render it impossible, or at least unfeasible, to be able to carry out comparative studies. Consequently we are, at the beginning of each investigation, placed in something of a dilemma.

As stated in Chapter 1, the approach of the scientific method to decision-making problems is unsurprising: namely, (1) a statement of the problem, (2) a collection of data and evidence, (3) formulation of a hypothesis, (4) testing of the hypothesis, (5) revision of the hypothesis, (6) further testing, (7) implementation, (8) testing of results from full implementation. We suggested in Chapter 3 that this process may be structured in flow-chart form.

All this is, of course, well accepted and well understood. As we have stated, however, it does beg a series of important questions. If we are going to 'solve' the model, we are faced with the problem of using the hypothesis as a way of deducing the likely consequences of different courses of action. In those cases in which we are seeking optimality, optimizing techniques, generally mathematical but often of a simulated form, are used in order to guide the decision-maker in his selection of a particular course of action. We observe, however, that at this stage other features creep in almost unnoticed.

We have already observed that there is no credit to be gained in science from failing to solve a problem. The scientist is a human being, and is anxious to obtain the regard of sceptical management and hence will tend to select problems which he knows he has a high probability of solving. Inevitably, in this selection he will be guided by his own past experience and by those areas in which he has worked, and hence we have seen certain operational research groups build up considerable experience and expertise in the handling of particular techniques. It appears that once a technique has been used successfully two or three times in a research group, there is considerable pressure on the memebrs of that group to continue using that technique even for problem areas in which it might not be fully appropriate. Operational research, as a whole, has been fortunate in that there are some groups with highly developed skills in linear programming, simulation, queueing theory and so on; but by formulating models in such a way that particular techniques of solution can be applied we have seen that there is another danger, namely that we may neglect the objectives and the objective function.

Objective free and objective constrained models

It is useful to survey some of the more common forms of techniques used in the solution of operational research problems and to comment on the way in which the techniques constrain the form of objectives that can be used.

Linear deterministic models rely completely on the important technique of linear programming. It is a technique which has assumed an importance in the literature, research and teaching, which is greater than its actual applicability and usefulness in practice. Linear programming imposes constraints in the form of linearity on the relationship between the controllable and uncontrollable variables within the model. It also imposes added linearity on the constraints, in the form of the inequalities which are imposed. There is also, of course, a complete linearity in the form of hte objective function. It is fortunate that accountants think mainly in linear terms, and hence the profit maximizing and cost minimizing functions which are so common in linear programming are acceptable to the accountant. There is much that can be said about the assumptions that can go into formulating a linear objective function for linear programming. It is sufficient, for our purposes, to say that there can be few operational researchers who have not felt slightly uneasy, at least, in the way in which linearity is imposed on the objective function. It is particularly easy to persuade management that they have linear objective functions for the reason given above, that all accounting processes are essentially linear relationships. It is, therefore, the case that in optimizing techniques, the objective function is virtually subsumed within the model. In addition, in those problems where one is not optimizing but obtaining a solution which is good enough, we shall find that although the functional relationship which has to be made 'good enough' rather than optimized, is linear and the variables enacted on are all constrained by linear relationships of one form or another, we still have a very serious constraint imposed on the form of objective functions which is used. Linear programming, therefore, is what might be termed a completely objective constrained approach.

As we saw in Chapters 6 and 7, the introduction of probabilities into functional relationships causes another set of difficulties. In investment the normal forms of risk analysis produce a result in the form of a probability profile. A normal temporal cash flow formulation, presented in deterministic form, is developed by risk analysis to replace a shape of a temporal profile of cash flow by the shape of a probability profile of some function of that cash flow. Not only does one have to ask whether one has improved the situation by simply replacing one profile with another but, much more importantly, until one is able to develop an idea of the utility of a particular probability profile, one is faced with the problem of persuading an executive to translate his objectives into the form of a single profile of probability. Hence, although risk analysis may appear objective free, it has severe constraints upon the form of objective function which can be solved by such an approach.

For the other forms of analysis used in such cases, such as decision trees, similar criticisms may be made. In a decision tree, as we have seen, one of the steps is to place some form of value at each of the end points of the tree. We have also seen that the utility of these end points to the decision-maker may change as he proceeds down the branches of the tree. Hence, in formulating a decision tree approach we are conditioning the decision-maker to have an objective function which is going to be probabilistic in nature, while constant in utility, a priori. This is a severe constraint.

Most operational researchers will be aware of the curious way in which one is committed to a form of objective function in the competitive problems which are treated by a game theoretic approach. The alternative methods assumed in gaming problems by which one would deduce an optimal policy, all have severe restraints imposed on them. The most severe restraint is their lack of realism. The selection of a game theoretic approach constrains the decision-maker to applying objective functions which are unrealistic in practice, merely for the sake of producing a situation which can be solvable by the methods of linear programming.

It will be noted that we have not mentioned one of the most widely used and most successful techniques for solving operational research problems, namely that of simulation. At first sight, simulation appears to be completely objective free. We must remember, however, that there are in general three main reasons for using a simulation approach, and these three reasons will each condition the usefulness of the answers we obtain from simulation. The first reason for using simulation, as in war gaming, is to carry out experimental work in those situations where we are denied real life experience. These are essentially problem situations of extrapolatory nature. In war gaming we are extrapolating both in time and in the knowledge of weapon systems. One of the most useful characteristics of simulation applied in these areas is that it is possible to deduce what effect as yet unknown weapon systems would have when applied in specific military situations. This is a very important way of showing the likely consequence of completing successfully particular pieces of research and development. In these uses of simulation it is often the case that the time taken to carry out the simulation it is often the case that the time taken to carry out the simulation experiments is greater than the real time of real life situations. This is because we have not succeeded in extracting from the real situation those elements of simplicity which enable real time to be accelerated. This is the case particularly where one is dealing with the human decision-maker, as one is with a general who may be acting as a commander in a war game.

The second reason for using simulation is that of induction. In marketing, for example, as we have seen, we may have formulated a hypothetical structure within a black box and we use the simulation to see whether the black box reacts like the real life it is imitating. To take an analogy we may produce a simulated bicycle to which we are going to apply a control process. We then have to use this simulated bicycle to see whether it performs and feels like a real life bicycle. This reason is one of the most rapidly growing in importance and opens up the whole area of the cybernetic approach to control.[4, 5]

The third reason for using simulation is to build on formal analytic relationships which have already been established, and to use them for rapid generation, in an experimental way, of the relationship between the controllable and the uncontrollable variables. This third reason is probably still the most widespread.

It is useful to comment on this last and third reason for using simulation. If we are to generate computerized results at a high speed, then unless we are going to lose the advantage of this speed we also have to find a way of classifying the results. These can either be classified very crudely into 'good' or 'bad', or at the very least we have to classify the results on a scale of measurement which is capable of judgement against the levels of the input variables. It is here that the danger lies. Once one has classified a variable by the extent to which it leads to 'good' or 'bad', one is committing oneself to being able to appeal to an objective function which is sufficiently clear-cut for rapid classification to take place.

All of the foregoing presupposes one very important consequence which has already been stated in this book. We hope we are belabouring the obvious. The consequence is, that we have to be very careful to spend as much time as we are allowed in understanding the problem with which we are dealing. One is occasionally horrified at the speed with which the operational researcher casts a complex problem into a particular model. We need time to understand the situation of management; we need time to understand the underlying technology of the situation (using technology in its broadest sense). We need time to be able to examine the constraints imposed on management action, and we need time to be able to examine whether the objectives of the organization should be recast. We may observe in passing that in those decision-making situations where management have had full knowledge of their performance, where they have had full knowledge of the way in which they are achieving a known objective, then in these situations it is often difficult, even by the use of the most sophisticated forms of mathematical and statistical analysis, to improve the performance by more than five per cent. It will certainly be the case, in these situations, that improvement in performance will only be gained, even to the extent of this five per cent, by formal mathematical analysis rather than straight-forward arithmetical measurement. The situations in which the greatest gain is achieved are those in which either something relevant is measured for the first time or, alternatively, those in which the organization is persuaded to work in a new way. For example, constraints imposed on management action may be removed. We may integrate the production functions of a number of different plants which have been working in competition with each other. All these removals of constraints may allow significant increases in effectiveness and efficiency. Nevertheless in those areas where we retain the objective and where we continue to accept the constraints laid down in the way in which the organization may operate, we would be deceiving ourselves and, more importantly, deceiving management if we estimated beforehand any greater pay-off than perhaps five per cent. The point is that most managers dealing with complex situations are dealing with them intelligently, within the boundaries imposed on them. The important conclusion to which we come from this, is that it may be a more effective use of the energy of the scientist to allow him to consider the form of the objective towards which the organization is straining, and also the form and nature of the constraints which are imposed on the way in which the company operates. If we can achieve a proper statement of objectives, if we can revise the constraints imposed on management action, then it is surely easier to allow the executive by his own trial and error process to get within the five per cent which he can always achieve. These points have been illustrated in a paper by the author[58] and have led him to formulate tentatively the law of the boundary condition:

'The optimal solution to a decision-making problem will be such that some, at least, of the constraints imposed on the decision-maker are operative. Hence an improved solution is possible if these constraints are relaxed. In special cases it might be that re-formulating the constraints means that the worst possible solution under the new conditions is an improvement on the best possible solution under the old. It may well be more sensible to allow management to find their own "best" solution under well formulated constraints than to force them to a disagreeable optimum under the old constraints.'

In summary therefore, the whole process of model building for decision-making is that first of all we should have an understanding of:

1. the basic motivations and pressures on all those working within the organization and the relationship between the organization and its environment;

2. an understanding of the technology of the situation, not only in terms of scientific and engineering technology but also in terms of the technology of communication and control which is available to management;

3. an understanding of the way in which the organization works, with particular reference to the form of solution which is likely to be applicable and usable on a day-to-day basis;

4. a consideration of the constraints which are imposed on the way in which management may work with particular understanding of those constraints which may be removable.

Within the light of the above understanding of the environment and situation of the organization we then have:

1. to state the objective or sets of objectives towards which the organization should be working and also to formulate ways of measuring the achievement of these objectives;

2. to state the set of causes and the set of possible effects which may stem from the causes, which will affect the degree of achievement of these objectives;

3. to formulate in logical connected fashion, if possible by means of a flow chart, the way in which these patterns of causes and patterns of effect might be expected to operate;

4. to classify this structure in ways which appear to be useful, so that one can have a rapid understanding and reference to similar successful solutions of this form of model. (As has been seen, we have suggested a simple classification into those model situations which incorporate feedback and those which do not. The main point is that the scientist should have formulated his own method for search of history to determine those similar situations which are likely to help him in the solution of the current problem.)

5. to collect data and opinions, in such a way as to clothe the logical statements of the model with numeracy and quantity;

6. having selected a particular technique for solution, to derive a solution of the model in terms of the particular set of controllable variables which should lead to an optimal solution or one that is satisfactory;

7. to examine this solution for robustness, namely explore the decision space and see which of the controllable and which of the uncontrollable variables are the most important in determining the sensitivity of the solution;

8. to examine the constraints imposed by management, in order to see which of them, if abandoned, would lead to significant improvements in performance;

9. to formulate a process for on-going control so that the solution, when implemented, may continue to be monitored in such a way that, when the level of the sensitive controllable or uncontrollable variables changes, either a new solution is calculated or, alternatively, another investigation is carried out to determine new optimal policies.

References

1. Toulmin, S. and Goodfield, J., *The Fabric of the Heavens*, Pelican, London, 1963.
2. Ackoff, R. L., *Scientific Method: Optimizing Applied Research Decisions*, John Wiley and Sons, New York, 1962.
3. Medawar, P., *The Art of the Soluble*, Methuen, London, 1967.
4. Beer, S., 'The World, The Flesh and the Metal', *Nature*, 205, No. 4968, January 16, 1965.
5. Beer, S., *Decision and Control*, John Wiley and Sons, London, 1966.
6. Machiavelli, *The Prince*, Pelican, London.
7. Ackoff, R. L., *A Concept of Corporate Planning*, John Wiley and Sons, New York, 1970.
8. Lipsey, R. G., *An Introduction to Positive Economics*, Weidenfield and Nicholson, U.K., 2nd Edition, 1966.
9. Rivett, B. H. P. and Ackoff, R. L., *A Manager's Guide to O.R.,* John Wiley and Sons, 1963.
10. Ackoff, R. L. and Sasieni, M. W., *Fundamentals of Operational Research*, John Wiley and Sons, New York, 1967.
11. Clapham, J. C. R. and Dunn, H. D., 'Communication in Collieries', *Proc. First Internat. Conf. on Oper. Res.*, E.U.P., London, 1957.
12. Ackoff, R. L., 'Operational accounting and operations research', *Journal of Accounting*, 99 (1955).
13. Churchman, C. W., *Prediction and Optimal Decision*, Prentice Hall, U.S.A., 1961.
14. Adelson, R. L., 'Capital Investment Criteria', *Operational Research Quarterly,* 16, 1, March 1965.
15. Hertz, D. B., *New Power for Management*, McGraw-Hill, New York, 1969.
16. Hertz, D. B., 'Risk Analysis in Capital Investment', *Harvard Business Review*, Jan.-Feb. 1964.
17. Hertz, D. B., 'Investment Policies that Pay Off', *Harvard Business Review*, Jan.-Feb. 1968.
18. Von Neumann, J. and Morganstern, O., *Theory of Games and Economic Behaviour*, Princeton University Press, Revised Edition 1953.
19. Rao, A. G., *Quantitative Theories in Advertising*, John Wiley and Sons, New York, 1970.
20. Emshoff, J. R. and Mercer, A., 'A Marketing Model for Sales to Consumers', *Operational Research Quarterly*, 18, 3, September 1967.
21. Mercer, A., 'Operational Marketing Research', *Journal Ind. Econ.*, 18, 1.
22. Schaffir, K. H., 'Operations Research in the Textile Industry', in Hertz, D. B. and Eddison, R. L. (Ed), *Progress in O.R. Vol. 2*, John Wiley and Sons, New York, 1964.
23. Hannsmann, F. and Rivett, B. H. P., 'Competitive Bidding', *Operational Research Quarterly*, 10, 1, March 1959, p. 49.

24. Stark, R. M., 'Competitive Bidding: A Comprehensive Bibliography', *Operations Research*, **19**, 2, March-April 1971.
25. Sharp, R. G. and Dando, M. R., *Decision Resource Management*, Sussex University 1977 (presented to 3rd International Metagame Conference, York University, Ontario, July 1977).
26. Berresford, A. and Dando, M. R., 'Operational Research for Strategic Decision-Making: the Role of World-View', *J.Opl.Res.Soc.*, **29**, 137-146, 1978.
27. Milburn, T. W., 'The Management of Crises', in C. F. Hermann (Ed.), *International Crises*, Free Press, New York, 1972.
28. Dixon, N. F., *On the Psychology of Military Incompetence*, Jonathan Cape, London, 1976.
29. Bennett, P. G., 'Toward a Theory of Hypergames', *Omega*, **5**, No. 6, 749-751, 1977.
30. Harsanyi, J. C., 'Games with Incomplete Information played by "Bayesian" players', *Management Science* **(A) 14** (i) 159, (ii) 320, (iii) 486, 1968.
31. Bennett, P. G. and Dando, M. R., 'Complex Strategic Analysis: a Hypergame Study of the Fall of France', *J.Opl. Res. Soc.*, 1979.
32. Rapoport, A., *Fights, Games and Debates*, Univ. of Michigan Press, 1960.
33. Luce, R. D. and Adams, E. W. 'The Determination of Subjective Characteristic Functions in Games with Misperceived Payoff Functions', *Econometrica*, **24**, 158-171, 1956.
34. Gregg, J. V. et al., *Mathematical Trend Curves; an aid to Forecasting*, Oliver and Boyd, London, 1964.
35. Coutie, G. A. et al., *Short Term Forecasting*, Oliver and Boyd, London, 1964.
36. Coen, P. et al., 'Lagged Relationships in Economic Forecasting', *Journal of the Royal Statistical Society*, Series A, 132, 133.
37. Leicester, C., *Britain in 2001 AD*, H.M.S.O., 1972.
38. Martel, *The Growth of Growth Fibres*, 9 April, 1977.
39. Freeman, C., Jahoda, M. and Miles, I., *Progress and Problems in Social Forecasting*, S.S.R.C., London, 1976.
40. Tocher, K. D., *The Art of Simulation*, E.U.P., London, 1964.
41. Sisson, R. L., 'Simulation: Uses' and Tocher, K. D., 'Simulation: Languages' in Aronofsky, J. S. (Ed.), *Progress in Operations Research*, Vol. III, John Wiley and Sons, New York, 1969.
42. Tocher, K. D. and Guest, G., 'The Control of Steel Flow', in Kraweras, G. and Morlat, G. (Eds.), *Proceedings of Third International Conference on Operational Research*, Dunod, Paris, 1964.
43. Thomas, C. J., 'The Genesis and Practice of Operational Gaming', in Davies, M. et al. (Eds.), *Proceedings of First International Conference on Operational Research*, E.U.P., London, 1957.
44. Hermann, C., 'Validation Problems in Games and Situations', *Behavioural Science*, **12**, 3 May 1967.
45. Goodeve, C. F., 'Science and Social Organisation', *Nature*, **188**, 4746, October 15, 1960.
46. Churchman, C. W. Ackoff, R. L. and Arnoff, E. L., *Introduction to Operational Research*, John Wiley and Sons, New York, 1957.
47. Gupta, S., *Choosing Between Multiple Objectives* (unpublished research paper), Management Science Center, University of Pennsylvania, 1969.
48. Rivett, B. H. P., 'Policy Selection by Structural Mapping', *Proc. R. Soc. Lond.*, **A.354**, 407-423 (1977).
49. Rivett, B. H. P. and Clarke, D., 'A Structural Mapping Approach to Complex Decision-Making' *J.Opl.Res.Soc.*, **29**, 2, pp. 113-128, 1978.
50. Rivett, B. H. P., 'Multidimension Scaling for Multiobjective Policies', *Omega*, **5**, No. 4, 1977.

51. Kruskal, J. B., 1964a. 'Multidimensional Scaling by Optimising Goodness of fit to non-metric hypothesis', *Psychometrika* 29, 1-27.
52. Kruskal, J. B., 1964b. 'Non-metric Multidimensional Scaling — A Numerical Method', *Psychometrika* 29, 28-42.
53. Kendall, D. G., 'Construction of Maps from 'Odd Bits of Information', *Nature, Lond.*, 231, 158-159, 1971.
54. Kendall, D. G., 'The Recovery of Structure from Fragmentary Information, *Phil. Trans.R.Soc.Lond.*, **A. 279**, 547-582, 1975.
55. Kendall, D. G. 1976b. 'Computer Techniques and the Archival Map Reconstruction of Mycenaean Messenia, *Proceedings of First Colloquium on Mycenaean Geography*, 1976.
56. Rivett, B. H. P., 'Indifference Mapping for Multiple Criteria Decisions'. To be published.
57. Rivett, B. H. P., 'Fitting a Decision Function to Multi Criteria Data'. To be published.
58. Rivett, B. H. P., 'Effecting Change in Stable Industrial Situations', *Operational Research Quarterly*, 13, 2, 1962.
59. Stevenson, R. L., *Eldorado, in Virginibus Purisque*, Chatton and Windus, London, (10th edn.), 1894.

Index